TESS OF THE D'URBERVILLES

First published in 1891, this book is still one of the most sensitive stories we have about the feelings of a young woman.

It is a very sad book: a young girl's life is slowly, but surely, destroyed – not by her enemies, but by the people who say they love her. What kind of love is this that destroys the thing it loves?

The sadness lies in watching the mistakes happen and being unable to stop them. Tess is a girl who overflows with happiness. Her life could be so happy – but the right man hesitates, and the wrong man finds her first. 'Don't let her go!' we want to shout, or 'Tell him now, before it's too late!'

But it is already too late: it happened a hundred years ago – it happens every day. And we can do nothing but watch as the great world turns, destroys Tess, and turns again . . . as if she had never existed.

THOMAS HARDY

Tess
of the d'Urbervilles

Retold by
Clare West

~

OXFORD UNIVERSITY PRESS

OXFORD
UNIVERSITY PRESS

Great Clarendon Street, Oxford OX2 6DP

Oxford University Press is a department of the University of Oxford.
It furthers the University's objective of excellence in research, scholarship,
and education by publishing worldwide in

Oxford New York

Auckland Cape Town Dar es Salaam Hong Kong Karachi
Kuala Lumpur Madrid Melbourne Mexico City Nairobi
New Delhi Shanghai Taipei Toronto

With offices in

Argentina Austria Brazil Chile Czech Republic France Greece
Guatemala Hungary Italy Japan Poland Portugal Singapore
South Korea Switzerland Thailand Turkey Ukraine Vietnam

OXFORD and OXFORD ENGLISH are registered trade marks of
Oxford University Press in the UK and in certain other countries

ISBN 978 0 19 479268 4

A complete recording of this Bookworms edition of
Tess of d'Urbervilles is available on audio CD ISBN 978 0 19 479248 6

Printed in Hong Kong

ACKNOWLEDGEMENTS

Photographs © Columbia Pictures Industries Inc.
The publishers would like to thank Columbia for their
kind permission to reproduce photographs

Word count (main text): 33,060 words

For more information on the Oxford Bookworms Library,
visit www.oup.com/bookworms

CONTENTS

The Maiden

1

One evening at the end of May a middle-aged man was walking home from Shaston to the village of Marlott in the Vale of Blackmoor. His legs were thin and weak, and he could not walk in a straight line. He had an empty egg-basket on his arm, and his hat was old and worn. After a while he passed an elderly parson riding a grey horse.

'Good night,' said the man with the basket.

'Good night, Sir John,' said the parson.

After another step or two the man stopped and turned round to speak to the parson.

'Now, sir, last market-day we met on this road at the same time, and I said "Good night" and you answered "Good night, Sir John", as you did just now.'

'I did,' said the parson.

'And once before that, almost a month ago.'

'I may have.'

'So why do you call me Sir John, when I am only John Durbeyfield?'

The parson rode nearer, and after a moment's hesitation, explained: 'It was because I've discovered something of historical interest. I am Parson Tringham, the historian. Do you really not know, Durbeyfield, that you are a direct descendant of the ancient and noble family of the d'Urbervilles? They descended from Sir Pagan d'Urberville, who came from Normandy with William the Conqueror in 1066.'

'Never heard that before, sir!'

'Well, it's true. Let me see your face. Yes, you have the

d'Urberville nose and chin. D'Urbervilles have owned land and served their King for hundreds of years. There have been many Sir Johns, and you could have been Sir John yourself.'

'Well!' exclaimed the man. 'And how long has this news about me been known, Parson Tringham?'

'Nobody knows about it at all,' said the parson. 'I just happened to discover it last spring, when I was trying to find out more about the d'Urbervilles and noticed your name in the village.'

'I've got an old silver spoon, and an old seal too at home,' said the man, wondering. 'So where do we d'Urbervilles live now, parson?'

'You don't live anywhere. You have died, as a noble family.'

'That's bad. So where do we lie?'

'In the churchyard at Kingsbere-sub-Greenhill.'

'And where are our family lands?'

'You haven't any.'

John Durbeyfield paused. 'And what should I do about it, sir?'

'Oh, nothing. It's a fact of historical interest, nothing more. Good night.'

'But you'll come and have some beer with me, Parson Tringham?'

'No, thank you, not this evening, Durbeyfield. You've had enough already.' The parson rode away, half regretting that he had told Durbeyfield of his discovery.

Durbeyfield walked on a few steps in a dream, then sat down with his basket. In a few minutes a boy appeared. Durbeyfield called to him.

'Boy! Take this basket! I want you to go and do something for me.'

The boy frowned. 'Who are you, John Durbeyfield, to order me about and call me "boy"? You know my name as well as I know yours!'

'Do you, do you? That's the secret! Well, Fred, I don't mind
telling you that the secret is that I'm one of a noble family.' And
Durbeyfield lay back comfortably on the grass. 'Sir John
d'Urberville, that's who I am. And I've got the family seal to
prove it!'

'Oh?'

'Now take up the basket, and tell them in the village to send a
horse and carriage to me immediately. Here's a shilling for you.'

This made a difference to the boy's view of the situation.

'Yes, Sir John. Thank you, Sir John.'

As they spoke, sounds of music came through the evening air
from the village.

'What's that?' said Durbeyfield. 'Have they heard my news
already?'

'It's the women dancing, Sir John.'

The boy went on his way and Durbeyfield lay waiting in the
evening sun. Nobody passed by for a long time, and he could
just hear the faint music in the distance.

The village of Marlott lies in the beautiful Vale of Blackmoor.
Although this valley is only four hours away from London, it
has not yet been discovered by tourists and artists. The best view
of the vale is from the hills surrounding it; it looks like a map
spread out. It is a quiet, sheltered part of the countryside, where
the fields are always green and the rivers never dry up. To the
south lies the great dividing line of hills. From here to the coast
the hills are open, the sun pours down on the huge dry fields, the
atmosphere is colourless. But here in the valley lies a completely
different countryside, smaller and more delicate. The fields are
tiny, the air makes you sleepy, the sky is of the deepest blue.
Everywhere you can see a rich greenery of grass and trees,
covering smaller hills and valleys. This is the Vale of Blackmoor.

And in the village of Marlott, following ancient custom,

In the village of Marlott, following ancient custom, the young women gathered to dance every holiday.

the young women gathered to dance every holiday. For this May-Day dance, all wore white dresses. There was a fine, handsome girl among them, with a red ribbon in her hair. As they danced, they noticed a carriage go by. Durbeyfield lay back in it, singing, 'I'm–Sir–John–and–I've–got–a–spoon–and–seal–and–my–family–lies–at–Kingsbere!' The girl with the ribbon, who was called Tess, turned red and said quickly to her friends, 'Father's tired, that's all.' The other girls just laughed but stopped when Tess looked unhappy. The dancing went on.

In the evening the men of the village came to watch and later to join the dancers. Three young strangers, who were passing by, also stopped to look. They explained they were brothers on a walking tour. The older two continued their walk, but the youngest seemed more interested in the girls than his brothers were, and stayed to dance with several of them. As he left the dance, he noticed Tess, who seemed a little sad that he had not chosen her. He looked back from the road, and could still see her in her white dress, standing modestly apart from the dancers. He wished he had danced with her. He wished he had asked her name. But it was too late. He hurried on to join his brothers.

The young stranger had made an impression on Tess. But soon, worried by her father's strange appearance that afternoon, she decided to walk home. After the excitement of the dance, her parents' small cottage was a depressing sight. It was dark inside, as they had only one candle. The furniture was old and worn. There were six children crowded into the tiny space. Their mother was doing the washing at the same time as putting the baby to sleep. Looking after so many children had aged Joan Durbeyfield, but she still showed some of her early prettiness, which Tess had inherited.

'Let me help with the washing, mother,' said Tess gently.

'Oh Tess, I'm glad you've come,' said her mother. 'There's something I must tell you.'

'Is it anything to do with father making such a fool of himself this afternoon?' asked Tess, frowning.

'That's all part of the excitement! They've discovered we're the oldest family in the whole county, going back a long way! And our real name is d'Urberville! Doesn't that make you proud! That's why your father rode home in the carriage, not because he'd been drinking, as people thought.'

'I'm glad of that. Will it do us any good, mother?'

'Oh yes! Great things may come of it. No doubt our noble relations will be arriving in their carriages as soon as they find out.'

'Where is father now?' asked Tess suddenly.

Her mother did not answer directly. 'He saw the doctor today, you know. It's fat round the heart, he says. That's the

cause of his illness. He might last ten years . . . might last ten
months or days.'

Tess looked anxious. Her father, suddenly a great man, to die
so soon! 'But where *is* father?' she asked firmly.

'Now don't you get angry!' said Mrs Durbeyfield. 'The poor
man was feeling so weak after the news that he went to
Rolliver's. He needs to build up his strength to deliver the
beehives tomorrow, remember.'

'Oh my God!' cried Tess. 'He went to a public house! And
you agreed to it, mother!'

'No, I didn't,' said Mrs Durbeyfield crossly. 'I've been waiting
for you to look after the children while I fetch him.'

Tess knew that her mother greatly looked forward to these
trips to Rolliver's. There she could sit by her husband's side
among the beer-drinkers, and forget that the children existed. It
was one of the few bright moments in her hardworking life. Mrs
Durbeyfield went out, and Tess was left with the children. They
were very young, and totally dependent on the Durbeyfield
couple: six helpless creatures who had not asked to be born at
all, much less to be part of the irresponsible Durbeyfield family.

2

It was eleven o'clock before all the family were in bed, and
two o'clock next morning was the latest time to set off with
the beehives. It was a distance of twenty or thirty miles on bad
roads to Casterbridge, where the Saturday market was held. At
half-past one Mrs Durbeyfield came into the bedroom where
Tess and all the children slept.

'The poor man can't go,' she whispered. Tess sat up in bed.

'But it's late for the bees already. We must take them today.'

'Maybe a young man would go?' asked Mrs Durbeyfield doubtfully. 'One of the ones dancing with you yesterday?'

'Oh no, not for the world!' said Tess proudly. 'And let everybody know the reason? I'd be so ashamed! I think *I* could go if little Abraham came with me.'

Tess and Abraham dressed, led out the old horse Prince with the loaded waggon, and set off in the dark. They cheered themselves up with bread and butter and conversation.

'Tess!' said Abraham, after a silence.

'Yes, Abraham.'

'Aren't you glad that we're a noble family?'

'Not particularly.'

'But you're glad you're going to marry a gentleman?'

'What?' said Tess, lifting her face.

'Our noble relations are going to help you marry a gentleman.'

'Me? Our noble relations? We haven't any. Whatever put that into your head?'

'I heard them talking about it at home. There's a rich lady of our family out at Trantridge, and mother said that if you claimed relationship with her, she'd help you marry a gentleman.'

His sister became suddenly silent. Abraham talked on, not noticing her lack of attention.

'Did you say the stars were worlds, Tess?'

'Yes.'

'All like ours?'

'They seem like our apples – most of them good, a few bad.'

'Which do we live on? A good one or a bad one?'

'A bad one.'

'If we lived on a good one, how would things be different?'

'Well, father wouldn't be ill and cough as he does, and mother wouldn't always be washing.'

'And you would have been a ready-made rich lady, and not have to marry a gentleman.'

'Oh, Aby, don't – don't talk of that any more!'

Abraham finally went to sleep on the waggon. Tess drove the horse. Gradually she fell into a dream. She could see her father, foolish in his pride, and the rich gentleman of her mother's imagination laughing at the poor Durbeyfield family.

Suddenly she awoke from her dream to noise and violent movement. Something terrible had happened. She jumped down and discovered that the post carriage, speeding along the dark road, had driven into her slow and unlighted waggon. Poor Prince was seriously hurt, and as she watched he fell to the ground.

'You were on the wrong side,' said the post driver. 'I must go on with the post, but I'll send somebody to help you as soon as I can. You'd better stay here with your waggon.'

He went on his way, while Tess stood and waited, tears pouring down her cheeks. Daylight came. Prince lay there, unmoving, his eyes half open.

'It's all my fault,' cried Tess. 'What will mother and father live on now? Aby, Aby, wake up! We can't go on with our beehives – Prince is dead!' When Aby realized what had happened, his face looked like an old man's.

'It's because we live on a bad star, isn't it, Tess?' he said through his tears.

Finally a man arrived with a horse, to take the waggon on to Casterbridge to deliver the beehives, and then collect Prince on the way back. When they got home, Tess broke the news to her parents. They were not angry with her, but she blamed herself completely.

When Durbeyfield heard he would only get a few shillings for Prince's dead body, he rose to the occasion.

'We d'Urbervilles don't sell our horses for cat's meat!' he insisted. And the following day he worked harder than usual in digging a grave, where Prince was buried. All the children cried.

'Has he gone to heaven?' asked Abraham in tears. But Tess did not cry. Her face was dry and pale. She felt she had murdered a friend.

3

Life now became rather difficult for the Durbeyfields. Without Prince to carry loads, John Durbeyfield could not buy and sell as he used to. He had never worked hard or regularly, and now he only occasionally felt like working. Tess wondered how she could help her parents. One day her mother made a suggestion.

'It's lucky we've found out about your noble blood, Tess. Do you know there's a very rich lady called Mrs d'Urberville living on the other side of the wood? She must be our relation. You must go to her and claim relationship with her, and ask for some help in our trouble.'

'I wouldn't like to do that,' said Tess. 'If there is such a lady, it would be enough to be friendly. We can't expect help from her.'

'*You* could persuade anybody, my dear. Besides, something else might happen. You never know.' And her mother nodded wisely.

'I'd rather try to get work,' said Tess sadly.

'What do you say, Durbeyfield?' said his wife, turning to him.

'I don't like my children asking for help,' said he proudly. 'I'm the head of the oldest branch of the family and a noble family like ours shouldn't have to ask for help.' Tess could not accept his reasons for not going.

'Well, as I killed the horse, mother, I suppose I ought to go. But don't start thinking about her finding a husband for me.'

'Who said I had such an idea?' asked Joan innocently.

'I know you, mother. But I'll go.'

Next morning Tess walked to Shaston, a town she hardly knew, and went on by waggon to Trantridge. The Vale of Blackmoor was her only world, and she had never been far outside the valley. All the knowledge she had came from her lessons in the village school, which she had left a year or two earlier. As soon as she left school she had tried to earn a little money by helping in the fields or milking cows or making butter. She blamed her mother for thoughtlessly producing so many children. Joan Durbeyfield was like a child herself, and never thought about the future. It was Tess who worried and worked and felt responsible for her little brothers and sisters. So naturally it was Tess who should represent her family at the d'Urberville home.

From Trantridge she walked up a hill, and turning a corner, saw the house. She stopped in amazement. It was large and almost new, a rich red against the green of the bushes around it. Behind it lay the woods called The Chase, an ancient forest. There were greenhouses and well-kept gardens. There was no lack of money here. Tess hesitated, almost frightened.

'I thought we were an old family!' she said to herself, 'but this is all new!' She wished she had not come.

She was right in a way. All this was owned by the d'Urbervilles, or the Stoke-d'Urbervilles as they called themselves at first. The Stokes were a northern business family who took an old-sounding name to add to their own when they moved into the south. So Tess was more of a d'Urberville than any of them, but did not know it.

A young man appeared in the garden. He looked about twenty-four, and was tall and dark, with full red lips and a black moustache curled at the ends.

'Well, my beauty, what can I do for you?' he said, looking interestedly at her. 'I'm Mr d'Urberville.'

It needed all Tess's courage to reply. 'I came to see your mother, sir.'

'I'm afraid you can't see her. She's ill. What do you want to see her about?'

'I . . . I . . . it seems so foolish!'

'Never mind,' said he kindly. 'I like foolish things. Try again, my dear.'

'I came, sir, to tell you we are of the same family as you.'

'Aha! Poor relations?'

'Yes.'

'Stokes?'

'No, d'Urbervilles.'

'Oh yes, of course, I mean d'Urbervilles.'

'We have several proofs that we are d'Urbervilles. We have an old silver spoon and a seal at home. But mother uses the spoon to stir the soup. Mother said we ought to tell you, as we are the oldest branch of the family and we've lost our horse in an accident.'

'Very kind of your mother,' said Alec d'Urberville, 'and I certainly don't regret it.' He looked admiringly at Tess, whose face blushed a deep pink. 'And so you've come on a friendly visit?'

'I suppose I have,' murmured Tess, looking uncomfortable.

'Let us walk round the gardens until you have to go home, my pretty cousin.' Tess wanted to leave as soon as possible, but the young man insisted. He took her to the greenhouses.

'Do you like strawberries?' he asked.

'Yes,' said Tess, 'when they are ready.'

'These are ready now,' and so saying, d'Urberville picked one and held it to her mouth.

'No no!' she said. 'I'd rather take it myself.'

But Alec put it into her mouth. He put roses into her hair and filled her basket with strawberries and flowers. He gave her food to eat, and watched her, while he quietly smoked a cigarette. She looked more adult and womanly than she really was. Alec could not take his eyes off her. She did not know as she smiled innocently at the flowers that behind the cigarette smoke was the cause of future sorrow in her life.

'What is your name?' asked Alec.

'Tess Durbeyfield. We live at Marlott.'

'I must see if my mother can find a place for you.' They said goodbye and she set off home carrying her strawberries and flowers.

This then was the beginning. Why did she have to meet the wrong man, and one who was so strongly attracted to her? Yet to the right man, she was only a half-forgotten impression from an evening's dancing in a country field. In life, the right man to love hardly ever comes at the right time for loving. Nature does not often answer a call for love, until the caller is tired of calling. In this case, as in millions, it was not the two halves of a perfect whole who met. A missing half wandered somewhere else, arriving much later. This delay was to have tragic results.

4

When Tess arrived home the following afternoon a letter had already been received by her mother. It appeared to come from Mrs d'Urberville, and offered Tess work looking after chickens. Joan Durbeyfield was delighted.

'It's just a way of getting you there without raising your hopes. She's going to recognize you as family, I'm sure of it.'

'I would rather stay here with father and you,' said Tess, looking out of the window.

'But why?'

'I'd rather not tell you, mother. I don't really know.'

A few days later when Tess came back from looking for work, the children came running out and danced round her.

'The gentleman's been here!' they shouted.

Joan was full of smiles. Mrs d'Urberville's son had called, and asked if Tess could come or not.

'He's a very handsome man!' said Mrs Durbeyfield.

'I don't think so,' said Tess coldly. 'I'll think it over.' She left the room.

'He's in love with her, you can see that,' said Mrs Durbeyfield to her husband. 'No doubt he'll marry her and she'll be a fine lady.'

John Durbeyfield had more pride in his new-found blood than energy or health. 'That's what young Mr d'Urberville is trying to do! Improve his blood by marrying into the old line!'

Persuaded by her mother and the children, Tess finally agreed to go. Mrs Durbeyfield secretly made wedding plans. Then the day came when Tess, wearing her best Sunday clothes on her mother's orders, said goodbye to her family.

'Goodbye, my girl,' said Sir John, waking from a short sleep.

The letter appeared to come from Mrs d'Urberville, and offered Tess work looking after chickens.

'Tell young d'Urberville I'll sell him the title, yes, sell it, at a reasonable price.'

'Not for less than a thousand pounds!' cried Lady Durbeyfield.

'No, tell him he can have it for a hundred! No, fifty, no – twenty! Yes, twenty pounds, that's the lowest. Family honour is family honour and I won't take any less!'

Tess felt like crying but turned quickly and went out. Her mother went with her to the edge of the village. There she stopped and stood waving goodbye, and watched her daughter walking away into the distance. A waggon came to take her bags, and then a fashionable little carriage appeared. It was driven by a well-dressed young man smoking a cigar. After a moment's hesitation, Tess stepped in.

Joan Durbeyfield, watching, wondered for the first time if she had been right in encouraging Tess to go. That night she said to her husband, 'Perhaps I should have found out how the gentleman really feels about her.'

'Yes, perhaps you ought,' murmured John, half asleep. Joan's natural trust in the future came back to her.

'Well, if he doesn't marry her before, he'll marry her after. If she plays her cards right.'

'If he knows about her d'Urberville blood, you mean?'

'No, stupid, if she shows him her pretty face.'

Meanwhile Alec d'Urberville was whipping his horse and driving the carriage faster and faster downhill. The trees rushed past at great speed. Tess was feeling thoroughly frightened. He took no notice when she asked him to slow down. She cried out and held on to his arm in fear.

'Don't touch my arm, hold on to my waist!' he shouted. At the top of another hill he said, laughing, 'Put your arms around me again, my beauty!'

'Never!' said Tess independently.

'Let me give you one little kiss, Tess, and I'll stop!'

'Will nothing else do?' cried Tess in despair. 'Oh, very well!'

As they raced on, he was on the point of kissing her, when she suddenly moved aside, so that he almost fell off.

'I'll break both our necks!' he swore passionately.

'I thought you would be kind to me,' said Tess, her eyes filling with tears. 'I don't want to kiss anybody!'

But he insisted, so in the end she sat still and d'Urberville kissed her. No sooner had he done so than she wiped the place on her cheek with her handkerchief. Just then her hat blew off into the road and d'Urberville stopped the horse. Tess jumped down to get it, then turned triumphantly to Alec.

'I shall walk from here,' she said firmly.

'But it's five or six miles more.'

'I don't care.'

'Let me give you one little kiss, Tess, and I'll stop!'
said Alec d'Urberville.

'You made that hat blow off on purpose! You did, didn't you?'

She was silent. He swore angrily at her.

'Don't use such bad words!' cried Tess. 'I shall go back to mother! I hate you!'

D'Urberville suddenly started laughing.

'Look, I promise never to do that again,' he said. 'Come, let me take you in the carriage.'

But she refused, and began to walk in the direction of Trantridge. So they progressed slowly, d'Urberville driving the carriage beside Tess.

5

The chickens for which Tess was responsible lived in an old cottage on Mrs d'Urberville's land. On her first day Tess had to take some of the chickens to show to their owner. She immediately realized the old lady was blind. Mrs d'Urberville held each bird and felt it carefully to see that it was in good health. At the end she suddenly asked Tess a question.

'Can you whistle?'

'Whistle, Ma'am?'

'Yes, whistle tunes. I want you to practise and whistle to my birds every day.'

'Yes, Ma'am.'

Tess was not surprised at Mrs d'Urberville's cold manner, and did not expect any more of such a great lady. However, she did not realize that the old lady had never even heard about the family connection.

Tess began to enjoy her new work with the chickens, and the next day in the cottage garden she decided to practise whistling as instructed. She was shocked to find that she had completely forgotten how to whistle. Suddenly she noticed a movement behind a tree near the wall. It was Alec d'Urberville.

'Well, cousin Tess,' he said, 'I've never seen such a beautiful thing as you! I've been watching you from over the wall. Look, I can give you a lesson or two.'

'Oh no you won't!' cried Tess, going back towards the door.

'Don't worry, I won't touch you. Just look . . .' and he showed her how to whistle. From that moment Tess found she could whistle tunes to the birds just as Mrs d'Urberville wanted. And as the weeks passed, she often met d'Urberville in the garden and began to lose her shyness of him.

Every Saturday night the other farm workers from the surrounding area used to go to drink and dance in the market town two or three miles away. On Sundays they would sleep late. For a long time Tess did not go with them. But after a while she wanted a change from her routine and began to go on the weekly trips regularly. She always came home with the others at night, preferring the protection of being in a group. One Saturday night she was in the town looking for her companions as it was time to go home, when she met Alec d'Urberville.

'What, my beauty? Here so late?' he said, smiling at her.

'I'm just waiting for my friends,' she answered.

'I'll see you again,' he said as she moved away.

She became worried when she realized the workers were still dancing wildly and would not be going home soon. Again she caught sight of Alec, waiting in a doorway, his cigar glowing red in the dark. Eventually she joined a group wandering home. They had all been drinking, but she felt safer with them than alone. But after a while she became involved in a quarrel with them, and was trying to get away from the angry group, when Alec d'Urberville rode by. He offered to take her home on the back of his horse. She hesitated, then accepted.

Together they rode along in the dark, Tess holding on to Alec. She was very tired: every day that week she had got up at five. So she did not notice that they were riding off the main road and into The Chase, the oldest wood in England. It began to get foggy, and finally Alec admitted honestly that he was lost.

'Put me down here, sir,' cried Tess at once. 'Let me walk home from here. How wrong of you to bring me away from the main road! I knew I shouldn't trust you!'

'Don't worry, my beauty,' laughed Alec. 'I thought you would enjoy a longer ride on such a lovely night. But I can't let you go. The fog is so bad now that you couldn't possibly find your way.

I'll leave you here and go to find out where we are. When I come back, I'll tell you, and you can come with me on horseback or go alone on foot – just as you like.'

She agreed to this. 'Shall I hold the horse?' she asked.

'No, he'll stay quiet,' answered Alec. 'By the way, your father has a new horse today. And the children have some new toys.'

'Was it . . . was it you who gave them? Oh, how good of you!' murmured Tess with a heavy heart. 'I almost wish you hadn't!'

'Tessy, don't you love me just a little now?'

'I'm grateful,' she admitted, 'but I'm afraid I don't . . .' and slowly she started to cry.

'Now don't cry, my dear. Sit here and wait for me.' He made a bed for the tired girl among the dead leaves, and covered her with his coat. He set off into the fog to find out where he was, and came back to find Tess fast asleep. He saw her in her white dress among the leaves, a pale, shining figure in the dark. He bent down and touched her cheek with his. Everywhere there was darkness and silence. The birds and animals slept, safe in and under the trees. But who was looking after Tess? Who was protecting her innocence?

'Tess!' said d'Urberville, and lay down beside her. The girl was not strong enough to resist him.

Why was Tess's girlish purity lost? Why does the wrong man take the wrong woman? Why do the bad so often ruin the good? Why is beauty damaged by ugliness? Thousands of years of philosophy cannot give us the answers to these questions. These things happen, and have always happened. Perhaps in the past, rolling home after a battle, Tess's ancestors, the real d'Urbervilles, had done the same, even more cruelly, to young country girls. But we cannot accept that that is Tess's fault, and should happen to her. As the people of her village say, 'It was to be.' And from now on, Tess's life was to be completely different.

Maiden No More

6

It was a Sunday morning in late October about four months after Tess's arrival at Trantridge, and a few weeks after the night ride in The Chase. Carrying a heavy basket and bundle, Tess was walking towards the hills which divided her from the Vale, her place of birth. The scenery and people on this side were very different from those in her village. Marlott people mainly thought and travelled northward and westward, while on this side people were interested in the east and the south. She walked up the same hill which d'Urberville had driven down so wildly that June day. On reaching the top of the hill, Tess paused and looked for a long time at the familiar green world of home. It was always beautiful from here, but since she had last seen it, her view of life had changed. She had learnt that wickedness exists, even where there is beauty, and now she could hardly bear to look down into the Vale.

Then she looked behind her and saw a carriage coming up the same hill that she had just climbed, with a man leading the horse. Soon he caught up with her.

'Why did you slip away in secret like that?' asked d'Urberville breathlessly. 'I've been driving like mad to catch up with you. Just look at my horse! You know nobody would have prevented you from going. I'm going to drive you the rest of the way, if you won't come back with me.'

'I won't come back,' she said quietly.

'I thought so! Well, let me help you up. Give me your basket.'

She stepped up into the carriage and sat beside him. She had no fear of him now. The reason for this was also the reason for her sorrow. They drove along, d'Urberville making conversation and Tess thinking her own thoughts. When they approached the village of Marlott a tear rolled down her cheek.

'Why are you crying?' he asked coldly.

'I was only thinking I was born over there.'

'Well, we must all be born somewhere.'

'I wish I had never been born, there or anywhere else!' she said quietly.

'Well, you shouldn't have come to Trantridge if you didn't want to. You didn't come for love of me, anyway.'

'That's quite true. If I had ever loved you, if I loved you still, I could not hate myself for my weakness as much as I do now.'

He did not look at her.

She added, 'I didn't understand your intention until it was too late.'

'That's what every woman says.'

'How dare you say that!' she cried angrily, her eyes flashing at him. 'My God! I could hit you! Did you never think that some women may not only say it but feel it?'

'All right,' he said laughing, 'I am sorry to hurt you. I did wrong – I admit it. Only don't keep accusing me. I am ready to pay for it. You need never work on the farms again.'

Her lip lifted slightly as she replied, 'I will not take anything from you! I cannot!'

'One would think you were a queen as well as being one of the real d'Urbervilles! Well, Tess dear, I suppose I'm a bad sort of man. I've always been one, and I always will be one. But I promise I won't be bad to you again. And if anything should happen – you understand – if you are in any trouble or need anything, just drop me a line and I'll send by return whatever you want.'

She stepped down from the carriage and was going to leave

him, when he stopped her and said, 'You're not going to turn away from me like that, dear? Come, let me kiss you!'

'If you wish,' she answered coldly. She offered her cool cheek to him, but her eyes rested on a distant tree as if the kiss had nothing to do with her.

'You don't give me your lips, Tess. I'm afraid you'll never love me.'

'It's true. I have never loved you, and I never can.' She added sadly, 'Perhaps I should tell a lie and then I could lead a comfortable life. But I have enough honour not to tell that lie. If I loved you, I might have a very good reason to tell you so. But I don't.'

Alec sighed heavily, as if this scene were depressing him.

'Well, you're very sad, Tess, and you have no reason to be. You're still the prettiest girl for miles around. Will you come back with me? Say you will!'

'Never, never! I've made up my mind, and I won't come.'

'Then goodbye!' and Alec jumped up into his carriage and drove off.

Tess did not watch him go, but continued her walk alone. It was still early in the day and the sun was not yet giving any warmth. Tess felt even sadder than the autumn sadness which surrounded her.

But soon a man came up behind her, a man with a pot of red paint in his hand.

'Good morning,' he said, and offered to carry her basket. 'You're up early on a Sunday,' he continued.

'Yes,' said Tess.

'A day of rest for most people, although *I* do more real work today than in the rest of the week put together.'

'Do you?'

'In the week I work for man, but on Sunday I work for God.

That's better work, don't you think? Wait a moment, I have something to do here.' He stopped at a gate, and in large red letters on the middle bar of the gate he painted some words from the Bible:

PUNISHMENT AWAITS YOU

In the soft air, against the gentle green of the trees and the peaceful fields, these great red words stared at Tess. They pointed a finger at her. This man was a stranger and could not know her story, but the words accused her.

'Do you believe what you paint?' she asked in a low voice.

'Do I believe those words? Do I believe I am alive!'

'But,' she whispered, trembling, 'suppose you were *forced* to do wrong?'

He shook his head. 'I can't answer that question. I paint the words and leave others to think about them in their own hearts.'

'I think they are horrible words!' cried Tess. 'I'll take my basket and go on now,' and she walked away from him, her heart beating fast. 'I don't believe God said those things!' she thought, as she reached her village.

There was smoke coming from her father's chimney, but seeing the inside of the cottage made her heart ache. It was as poor as ever. Her mother jumped up, surprised to see her.

'Well, my dear Tess!' she said, kissing her. 'How are you? Have you come home to be married?'

'No, not for that, mother.'

'What, isn't your cousin going to marry you?'

'He's not my cousin, and he's not going to marry me.'

Her mother looked at her closely. 'Come, you haven't told me everything.'

Then Tess went up to her mother, put her head on Joan's shoulder, and told her the whole story.

'And you haven't persuaded him to marry you!' cried Joan. 'What's the good of going there? Why didn't you think of doing some good for your family instead of thinking only of yourself?'

Tess was confused. Alec had never mentioned marriage to her. But even if he had, she would never have accepted him, because she did not love him. This made her hate herself for what she had done. She would certainly never love him in the future. She did not quite hate him, but did not wish to marry him, even to remain respectable.

'You ought to have been more careful if you didn't want to marry him!'

'Oh mother!' cried the poor girl, her heart breaking. 'Why didn't you warn me about men? I was a child when I left home! I didn't know how dangerous they can be, and you didn't tell me!'

'Well, we must make the best of it,' said her mother. 'It's only human nature, after all.'

That afternoon the little cottage was full of Tess's friends, girls who lived in the village and who had missed her while she had been away. They whispered to each other that Tess was sure to marry that handsome gentleman. Fortunately Tess did not hear them. She joined in their laughing and talking, and for a short time almost forgot her shame.

But the next day was Monday, the beginning of the working week, when there were no best clothes and no visitors. She awoke with the innocent children asleep around her, she who had lost her innocence. She looked into her future, and grew very depressed. She knew she had to travel on a long, stony road, without help or sympathy. She had nothing to look forward to, and she wanted to die.

In the next few weeks, however, she became more cheerful, and went to church one Sunday morning. She loved listening to the well-known tunes, and gave herself up to the beauty of the music. She wondered at the composer's power. From the grave he could make a girl like her, who had never known him, feel extremes of emotion. She sat in a quiet, dark corner listening to the service. But when the village people arrived at church they noticed her and started whispering to each other. She knew what they were saying and realized she could come to church no more.

So she spent almost all her time in her bedroom, which she shared with the children. From here she watched the wind, the snow, the rain, beautiful sunsets and full moons, one after another. People began to think she had gone away. She only went out after dark, to walk in the woods and the fields. She was not afraid of the dark or the shadows; it was people she was anxious to avoid. She was at home on the lonely hills, but she felt guilty surrounded by innocent nature. When it rained, she thought nature was crying at her weakness, and when the midnight wind blew she thought nature was angry with her. But she did not realize that although she had broken an accepted social rule, she had done nothing against nature. She was as innocent as the sleeping birds in the trees, or the small field animals in the hedges.

7

One day in August the sun was rising through the mist. In a yellow cornfield near Marlott village it shone on two large arms of painted wood. These, with two others below, formed the turning cross of the reaping-machine. It was ready for today's harvest. A group of men and a group of women came down the road at sunrise. As they walked along, their heads were in the sun while their feet were in the shadow of the hedge. They went into the field.

Soon there came a sound like the love-making of the grasshopper. The machine had begun, and three horses pulled it slowly along the field. Its arms turned, bright in the sunlight. Gradually the area of standing corn was reduced. So was the living space of the small field animals, who crowded together, not knowing that they could not escape the machine in the end.

The harvesters followed the machine, picking and tying up bundles of corn. The girls were perhaps more interesting to look at. They wore large cotton hats to keep off the sun, and gloves to protect their hands from the corn. The prettiest was the one in the pale pink jacket, who never looked around her as she worked. She moved forward, bending and tying like a machine. Occasionally she stood up to rest. Then her face could be seen: a lovely young face, with deep dark eyes and long heavy curling hair. Her cheeks were paler, her teeth more regular, and her red lips thinner than most country girls'.

It was Tess Durbeyfield, or d'Urberville, rather changed, living as a stranger in her home village. She had decided to do outdoor work and earn a little money in the harvest.

The work continued all morning, and Tess began to glance towards the hill. At eleven o'clock a group of children came over the hill. Tess blushed a little, but still did not pause in her work. The eldest child carried in her arms a baby in long clothes. Another brought some lunch. The harvesters stopped work, sat down and started to eat and drink.

Tess also sat down, some way from the others. She called the girl, her sister, and took the baby from her. Unfastening her dress, and still blushing, she began feeding her child. The men kindly turned away, some of them beginning to smoke. All the

'She loves that child, though she says she hates him and wishes they were both dead.'

other women started to talk and rearrange their hair. When the baby had finished Tess played with him without showing much enthusiasm. Then suddenly she kissed him again and again, as if she could not stop. The baby cried out at the violence of her kisses.

'She loves that child, though she says she hates him and wishes they were both dead,' said one of the women, watching the young mother.

'She'll soon stop saying that,' replied another. 'She'll get used to it. It happens to lots of girls.'

'Well, it wasn't her fault. She was forced into it that night in The Chase. People heard her sobbing. A certain gentleman might have been punished if somebody had passed by and seen them.'

'It was a pity it happened to her, the prettiest in the village.

But that's how it happens! The ugly ones are as safe as houses, aren't they, Jenny?' and the speaker turned to one who was certainly not beautiful.

Tess sat there, unaware of their conversation. Her mouth was like a flower, and her eyes were large and soft, sometimes black, blue or grey, sometimes all three colours together. She had spent months regretting her experience and crying over it, but suddenly decided that the past was the past. In a few years her shame, and she herself, would be forgotten. Meanwhile the trees were just as green, and the sun shone just as brightly, as before. Life went on.

She most feared what people thought of her, and imagined that they talked constantly about her behind her back. In fact she was not often discussed, and even her friends only thought about her occasionally. Other things of more importance took up their time. If there had been no people around her, Tess would not have made herself so unhappy. She would have accepted the situation as it was. She was miserable, not because she felt unhappy, but because she imagined herself rejected by society.

Now she wanted to be useful again, and to work. So she dressed neatly, and helped in the harvest, and looked people calmly in the face, even when holding her baby in her arms.

Having eaten her lunch quickly, Tess went back to work with the harvesters in the cornfield until it was dark. They all came home on one of the largest waggons, singing and laughing together.

But when Tess reached home, she discovered that the baby had fallen ill that afternoon. He was so small and weak that illness was to be expected, but this still came as a shock to Tess. She forgot the shame surrounding his birth, and only wished passionately to keep him alive. However, it became clear that he was dying. Now Tess had a greater problem. Her baby had not been baptized.

Her ideas on religion were not very developed. She had more or less accepted that she would go to hell for her crime, and did not much care what would happen to her after death. But for her baby it was different. He was dying, and must be saved from hell.

It was nearly bedtime, but she rushed downstairs and asked if she could send for the parson. Her father had just returned from the public house, and was at his most sensitive to the shame brought upon his noble name by Tess. He refused to allow the parson in, and locked the door.

The family went to sleep. As the night passed, Tess realized, in great misery, that the baby was close to death. She walked feverishly up and down the room, until an idea came to her.

'Ah! Perhaps baby can be saved! Perhaps it will be just the same!'

She lit a candle, and woke her young brothers and sisters. Having poured some water into a bowl, she made them kneel around, with their hands together as in church. The children were hardly awake and watched Tess with big round eyes.

She looked tall in her long white nightdress, her long dark hair hanging down her back to her waist. Her enthusiasm lit up her face, giving it a beautiful purity – the face which had caused her shame.

She picked up the baby. One of the children asked, 'Are you really going to baptize him, Tess? What's his name going to be?'

She had not thought of that, but remembered the story of Adam and Eve in the Bible. Because they did wrong together, God said they would live in sorrow for the rest of their lives.

She said firmly, 'SORROW, I baptize you in the name of the Father, and of the Son, and of the Holy Ghost.'

She splashed some water on the child, and there was silence.
'Say Amen, children.'

'Amen,' they replied.

Tess put her hand into the water, and drew a huge cross upon the baby with her finger. She continued the service in the well-known words, asking for the baby to be protected against the world and against wickedness. Her belief gave her hope; her sweet warm voice rang out the thanks that follow the baptism. The single candle was reflected in her shining eyes like a diamond. The children asked no more questions, but looked up at her in amazement. She seemed almost like a god to them.

Poor Sorrow's fight against the world and wickedness was a short one, fortunately perhaps, taking into account his situation. In the blue light of the morning he breathed his last. Tess had been calm since the baptism and she remained calm. She was no longer worried about Sorrow's afterlife. If God did not accept the baptism, she did not value His Heaven, either for herself or for her child.

Tess thought a good deal about the baptism, however, and wondered if it might mean that Sorrow could be buried in the churchyard, with a church service. She went to the parson's house after dark, and met him near his gate.

'I should like to ask you something, sir. My baby was very ill, and I wanted you to baptize him, but my father refused to allow it. So I baptized him myself. Now sir, can you tell me this,' and she looked him straight in the eyes, 'will it be just the same for him as if you had baptized him?'

The parson wanted to say no. She had done what should have been his job. But the girl's strong feeling impressed him. The man and the parson fought inside him, and the man won.

'My dear girl,' he said, 'it will be just the same.'

'Then will you bury him in the churchyard?' she asked quickly.

The parson felt trapped. It was a difficult question to answer. 'Ah, that's a different matter,' he said. 'I'm sorry, I cannot.'

'Oh sir!' She took his hand as she spoke.

He took it away, shaking his head.

'Then I'll never come to church again!' she cried. 'But perhaps it will be the same for him? Tell me, have pity on me, poor me, tell me what you really think!'

The parson was deeply touched by her emotion. For a surprising moment he forgot the strict rules of his church.

'It will be just the same,' he answered kindly.

So the baby was carried in a cheap wooden box to the churchyard at night. There is a corner of the churchyard where the grass grows long, and where the suicides, drunks, unbaptized babies and other supposed criminals are laid. Sorrow was buried here, at the cost of a shilling and a pint of beer for the gravedigger. Tess bravely made a little cross and put it at the head of the grave one evening, when she could enter the churchyard without being seen.

It is all very well saying that we learn from experience. Tess had certainly learnt from experience, but could not see how to use her knowledge, so painfully gained.

So she stayed in her parents' home during the winter, helping to look after the children, making clothes for them and earning a little money whenever she could. Important dates came round again: the night of her shame in The Chase, the baby's birth and death, her own birthday. One day when she was looking at her pretty face in the mirror, she thought of another date, even more important – her own death. When it came it would swallow up all her prettiness and everything that had happened to her. When was it? It was a day lying hidden among all the other days of the year, so that she noticed nothing when it came round, and did not know what week, month, season or year it would be.

In a flash Tess changed from simple girl to complicated woman. Her face was often thoughtful, and there was sometimes a tragic note in her voice. Her eyes grew larger and more expressive. She became a beautiful woman. She had suffered, but had gained a certain self-confidence from her experiences.

Although the village people had almost forgotten her trouble, she decided she could never be really happy in Marlott. Trying to claim relationship with the rich d'Urbervilles seemed so foolish and shameful to her. She thought her family would never be respected there again. Even now she felt hope rise within her, hope of finding a place with no family connections and no memories. In escaping from Marlott she intended to destroy the past. Perhaps now she could make up for her crime against society.

Consequently she looked hard for work away from Marlott. She finally heard that a dairyman some miles to the south needed a good milkmaid for the summer. Having decided to go there, she promised herself there would be no more hopeless dreams. She would simply be the dairymaid Tess, and nothing more. Even her mother no longer talked about their connection with the noble d'Urbervilles.

But in spite of Tess's decision to forget her ancestors, the dairy, called Talbothays, especially attracted her because it was near the former lands of the old d'Urberville family. She would be able to look at them, and not only observe that the noble d'Urberville family had lost its greatness, but also remember that a poor descendant had lost her innocence. She wondered if some good might come of being in the land of her ancestors. Hope and youthful energy rose up in her again, like leaves on a young tree in spring.

A New Life

8

And so it was that on a beautiful morning in May, two to three years after her return from Trantridge, Tess Durbeyfield left home for the second time. She was going in the opposite direction this time. When she reached the first hill, she looked back at Marlott and her father's house with sadness in her heart.

She travelled partly by carriage and partly on foot, carrying her basket. Not far to her left she could see the trees which surrounded Kingsbere, with its church where her ancestors lay in their tombs. She could no longer admire or respect them. She almost hated them for ruining her life. Nothing of theirs was left except the old seal and spoon.

'Huh! I have as much of mother as father in me!' she said. 'All my prettiness comes from her, and she was only a dairymaid.'

Her walk took two hours, until she reached the hill overlooking the Valley of the Great Dairies. This valley was watered by the river Froom, and produced huge amounts of milk and butter, more even than Tess's Vale of Blackmoor, which was known as the Vale of Little Dairies.

As she stood and looked, she realized the valleys were quite different. Here the fields and farms were much larger. She saw more cows at a glance than she had ever seen before. The evening sun shone on their red, white and brown bodies. She thought that this view was perhaps not as beautiful as a view of Blackmoor Vale, which she knew so well. There the sky was deep blue, the smell of the earth was heavy in the air, the streams ran slowly and silently. But this view was more cheerful. Here the air was clear and light, and the river Froom rushed as fast as the shadow of a cloud.

Either the change in the quality of the air, or the feeling that she was going to start a new life here, made her feel much happier. She ran along, her hopes and the sunshine warming her.

She looked at her best as she ran laughing into the warm wind. The desire for pleasure, which is in every living thing, had finally won over Tess. She was, after all, only a young woman of twenty, who had not finished growing up. No event, however unpleasant, could have marked her for ever. She was young and strong and beautiful, and could not remain sad for long.

Her hopes rose higher than ever. She wanted to show how grateful she was for this second chance. She started singing love songs, but found they were not enough to express her feelings. She remembered the Sunday mornings of her girlhood, and sang: 'Oh sun and moon ... Oh stars ... Oh children of men ... Praise the Lord! Praise Him for ever!' until she stopped suddenly and murmured, 'But perhaps I don't quite know the Lord yet.'

This was probably a pagan feeling in a religious form. People who live in the country and are close to nature, like Tess, keep many of the pagan ideas of their ancestors in their souls. Religion learned in church comes much later, and does not touch them deeply.

Tess was happy to be making her way independently in life. She really wanted to live honestly and work hard, unlike her father. Tess had her mother's energy and the energy of her youth to help her recover from her experience. Women do usually live through such experiences. 'Where there's life there's hope' is still true for most 'betrayed' women.

As Tess, full of enthusiasm, came downhill towards the dairy, she suddenly heard the milking call, again and again, from all parts of the valley. It was half-past four, when the dairy people brought in the cows. Tess followed the red and white animals, with their great bags of milk under them, into the farmyard. She saw the long sheds, and the wooden posts, shining and smooth where the cows had rubbed against them over the years. She saw the cows between the posts, the sun throwing their shadows on the wall as carefully as a painter paints a beautiful king or queen. As the cows waited for their turn, the milk fell in drops on the ground.

The dairymaids and men had come from their cottages as they saw the cows arriving from the fields. Each girl sat on her three-legged stool as she milked, her right cheek resting on the cow's body, watching Tess arrive. The men milked with their hats low over their eyes and did not see her. One of them was a middle-aged man, the head-dairyman she was looking for. He worked six days a week in his white milking clothes, milking and butter-making, and on the seventh he wore his best suit to take his family proudly to church. Because of this people nearby used to say:

Dairyman Dick
All the week,
On Sundays Mister Richard Crick.

Most dairymen are usually bad-tempered at milking time, but Mr Crick was glad to get a new dairymaid at this busy time of the year. So he received Tess warmly and asked her how her family were.

'When I was a boy I knew your part of the country very well,' he said. 'An old woman of ninety – she's dead now but she used to live near here – she once told me there was an ancient noble family of a name like yours, who came from here originally. But I didn't take any notice of an old woman like that.'

'Oh no, that's just a story,' said Tess.

Then Mr Crick turned to business. 'You can milk well, my girl? I don't want my cows drying up, especially just now.'

'Oh yes, I can,' answered Tess.

He looked at her delicate hands and pale face.

'Quite sure you're strong enough for this sort of life? It's comfortable enough here for rough country people but it's hard work.'

'Oh yes, I'm strong enough. I'm used to hard work,' Tess insisted.

'Well, have some tea and something to eat. You've had a long journey,' he said kindly.

'No, I'd rather begin milking straight away,' said Tess. 'I'll just drink a little milk first.'

This surprised Dairyman Crick, who appeared never to have thought of milk as a drink.

'Oh, if you can swallow it, have some,' he said, holding the bucket for her to drink from. 'I haven't touched any for years. It would lie in my stomach like a stone, so it would. Now, try that one and see how you get on.' And he pointed to the nearest cow.

As soon as Tess was on her stool under the cow, and the milk was pouring between her fingers into the bucket, she really felt that her new life was beginning. As she relaxed, she looked around her.

It was a large dairy. There were nearly a hundred milking cows. Dairyman Crick milked six or eight of the difficult ones with his own hands. He could not trust them to the dairymaids, because if the cows were badly milked their milk would simply dry up.

For a while there was no more talk among the milkers. Suddenly Mr Crick got up from his stool.

'We're not getting as much milk from them as usual,' he said. 'We'd better sing them a song, friends, that's the only thing to do.' So the group of milkers started singing, to encourage the cows to give more.

Mr Crick went on, 'But I think bulls like music better than cows. Did I tell you all about William Dewy? On his way home after a wedding he found himself in a field with an angry bull. He took his violin and played some Christmas church music and down went the bull on his knees! Just like the animals around baby Jesus! And so William was able to escape.'

'It's a curious story. It takes us back to the past, when belief in God was a living thing.' This unusual remark came from under a cow.

'Well, it's quite true, sir, believe it or not. I knew the man well,' said Mr Crick.

'Oh yes, I'm sure it's true,' said the man behind the brown cow. Tess could not see his face, and could not understand why the head-dairyman himself should call him sir. The man stayed under the cow long enough to milk three, at times saying something angrily to himself. Then he stood up, stretching his arms. Tess could now see him clearly. He wore the clothes of a dairyman but underneath he was quite different. He looked educated and gentlemanly.

But now she realized that she had seen him before. He was one of the three walking brothers who had stopped their walk to admire the May-Day dance in Marlott a few years before. He had danced with some of the other girls but not with her. He had not noticed her and had gone on his way. For a moment she was worried that if he recognized her he might discover her story. But she soon saw he did not remember her at all. Since she had seen him in Marlott, his face had grown more thoughtful. He now had a young man's moustache and beard. From the time he had spent milking one cow, he was clearly a beginner at dairy work.

Tess discovered that only two or three of the dairymaids slept in the house, besides herself. They all shared a big bedroom near the cheese room. That night one of the girls insisted on telling Tess about all the people at the dairy. To Tess, half asleep, the whispers seemed to be floating in the air.

'Mr Angel Clare – he's the one who's learning milking – he's a parson's son and thinks a lot and doesn't notice girls. His father is parson at Emminster, some way from here. His sons, except Mr Clare, are going to be parsons too.'

Tess gradually fell asleep.

9

Neither Angel Clare nor his family had originally chosen farming as a profession for him. When he was a boy, people admired his great qualities. Now he was a man, something vague and undecided in his look showed that he had no particular purpose in life. He was the youngest son of a poor parson. One day when he was studying at home, his father discovered that Angel had ordered a book of philosophy, which questioned the Church's teaching. How could his son become a priest if he read such books? Angel explained that he did not in fact wish to enter the Church like his brothers, because the Church's views were too strict and did not allow free thinking. The simple parson was shocked. He was a man of fixed ideas and a firm believer. And if Angel did not want to become a priest, what was the use of sending him to study at Cambridge? For the parson the whole point of going to university was to become a minister of God.

'I want to use my mind,' Angel insisted. 'I want to read philosophy. I want to question my belief, so that what is left after I have questioned it, will be even stronger.'

'But Angel, your mother and I have saved and saved to send you to university like your brothers. But how can we send you there if it is not in the service of God?'

So Angel did not have the advantage of a university education. After some years studying at home he decided to learn farming. He thought this kind of work could give him what he most valued, independence and freedom to think. So he came to Talbothays at twenty-six, as a student.

At first he stayed up in his room most of the time in the evenings, reading and playing his harp. But he soon preferred to read human nature by taking his meals in the general dining-room with the dairy people. The longer he stayed, the more Clare liked living with these simple country people. No longer did he see them as lacking in intelligence. He realized they were no different from him: he and they were all people walking on the dusty road which ends in death. He began to like working outside. He was learning about nature and about life. He came to know the changing seasons, morning and evening, different winds, waters and mists, shade and silence, and the voices of nature. All this he had never known before.

For several days after Tess's arrival, Clare, sitting reading a book, hardly noticed she was there. But one morning at breakfast he was reading music and listening to the tune in his head, when he heard a musical voice which seemed to become part of his tune. He looked round at Tess, seated at the table.

'What a fresh and pure daughter of nature that dairymaid is!' thought Angel. He seemed to remember something about her, something which took him back into a happy past, before decision made his life difficult. This memory made him look more often at Tess than the other dairymaids.

10

Dairyman Crick insisted that all the dairy people should milk different cows every day, not just their favourites. He was worried that a dairymaid might leave the dairy, and then her cows would not like being milked by a stranger. However, Tess began to find that the cows which came to her usually happened to be her favourites. This made her milking much easier. But she soon realized that it was not by chance, as it was Angel Clare who sent the cows in for milking.

'Mr Clare, you have sent me my favourite cows!' she accused him one morning, blushing.

'Well, it doesn't matter,' said he. 'You will always be here to milk them.'

'Do you think so? I hope I shall. But I don't know.' Afterwards she was angry with herself. She had spoken too seriously to him, as if he were involved in her staying or leaving. In the evening after milking she walked in the garden alone, thinking about it.

It was a typical summer evening in June. The air was delicate and there was a complete, absolute silence. It was broken by the sound of a harp. The notes floated in the still air, strong and clear. Tess listened like a fascinated bird. She drew near to

Clare, who still had not seen her. She was conscious of neither time nor space. The tune moved through her mind and body, bringing tears to her eyes. The waves of colour of the wild flowers mixed with the waves of sound. Angel finished playing, and caught sight of her. She blushed and moved away.

'Why are you going, Tess?' he asked. 'Are you afraid?'

'Oh no, sir, not of outdoor things.'

'But indoors?'

'Well, yes, sir.'

'Life in general?'

'Yes, sir.'

'Ah, so am I, very often. Being alive is rather serious, don't you think so?'

'It is, now you put it like that.'

'All the same, I wouldn't expect a young girl like you to feel that. Why? Come, tell me.'

After a moment's hesitation she answered, 'The trees ask questions with their eyes, don't they? And you seem to see hundreds of tomorrows all in a line, the first big and clear, the others getting smaller. But they all look fierce and cruel. But you can drive away all these ideas with your music, sir!'

He was surprised to find that this dairymaid had such sad thoughts. She was expressing in her own words the ache of modern life. This sadness made her more interesting to him. He did not know that her experience had given her great strength of feeling. Tess, on the other hand, could not understand why a man of religious family, good education and financial independence should feel sorry to be alive. How could this admirable and poetic man have felt, as she did two or three years ago, that he would rather die? It was true that he was not at present living among gentlemen. But he was studying what he wanted to know, and would become a rich farmer in time. So, as they neither understood each other's secrets, they were both puzzled and waited to find out more.

At first Tess regarded Angel as an intelligence rather than a man. She became quite depressed as she realized the distance between her own knowledge and his. One day he asked her why she looked so sad.

'Oh, it's only that I feel I've been wasting my life! When I see what you know, I feel what a nothing I am!'

'Well, my dear Tess,' said Angel with some enthusiasm, 'I shall be only too glad to help you study history, for example . . .'

'I don't know. What's the use of learning that I'm one of a long row, and that my past and future are like thousands of other people's? But there's one thing I'd like to know – why the sun shines on the good and the bad just the same,' she said, her voice trembling.

'Oh, Tess, don't be bitter!' Of course he had wondered this himself in the past. But as he looked at her innocent lips, he thought this pure child of nature could only have picked up the question from others. She could not possibly have any guilt in her past.

When he had gone, Tess felt again how stupid she must appear to him. She wondered whether she could gain his respect by telling him of her d'Urberville blood. She first asked the dairyman if Mr Clare was interested in old families who had lost their money and land.

'No,' said Mr Crick firmly. 'He's a rebel, and the one thing he hates is an old family.' After hearing this not very accurate view of Clare's opinions, poor Tess was glad she had not mentioned her ancestors.

That summer, Tess and Clare unconsciously studied each other, balanced on the edge of a passion, yet just keeping out of it. But all the time, like two streams in a valley, they were destined to join. Tess had never been so happy as she was now, and perhaps never would be so again. They met continually. They could not help it. They met daily in the half-light, at three o'clock in the morning, just before milking. They felt they were the first two up in the whole world, like Adam and Eve. Tess seemed like a queen to Clare, perhaps because he knew that she was the most beautiful woman walking about at this time of day. Lovely women are usually asleep at midsummer sunrise. But Tess was near, and the rest were nowhere. In the strange light she was no longer a milkmaid, but a vision of woman, the whole of womanhood in one form.

One day just after breakfast they all gathered in the milkhouse. The milk was turning in the churn, but the butter would not come. Dairyman Crick was worried.

'Maybe someone in the house is in love,' suggested his wife. 'That sometimes causes it. D'you remember that maid years ago, and the butter didn't come . . . ?'

'Ah yes, but that wasn't being in love,' replied Mr Crick. 'That was damage to the churn.' He turned to Clare to tell the story.

'Jack Dollop, one of our milkers, got a girl into trouble. One day her mother came looking for him with a great heavy umbrella in her hand. Jack hid in the churn, but she found him and turned it round and round. "Stop, stop!" cried Jack. "If you promise to marry my daughter!" shouted the mother. And so he did.'

Tess, very pale, had gone to the door for some fresh air. Fortunately the butter suddenly came. But Tess remained depressed all afternoon. To the others the story was funny. She alone could see the sorrow in it, and it reminded her of her experience.

Tess was first in bed that night, and was half asleep as the other girls undressed. She saw them standing at the window looking at someone in the garden with great interest.

'It's no use you being in love with him any more than me, Retty Priddle,' said Marian, the eldest.

'There he is again!' cried Izz Huett, a pale girl with dark hair.

'I would just marry him tomorrow if he asked me,' said Marian, blushing.

'So would I, and more,' murmured Izz.

'And I too,' whispered Retty shyly.

'We can't all marry him,' said Izz.

'We can't anyway,' said Marian. 'He likes Tess Durbeyfield best. I've watched him every day and found it out.'

There was a thoughtful silence.

'How silly this all is!' said Izz impatiently. 'He's a gentleman's son. He won't marry any of us or Tess either!' They all sighed, and crept into their beds, and fell asleep. But Tess, with her deeper feelings, could not sleep. She knew Angel Clare preferred her to the others. She was more attractive, better educated and more womanly. She could keep his affection for her. But should she? Perhaps the others should have a chance of attracting his attention, and even of marrying him. She had heard from Mrs Crick that Mr Clare had spoken of marrying a country girl to help him farm, milk cows and reap corn. Tess had promised herself she would never marry and would never be tempted to do so. She ought to leave the field open for the other girls.

Next morning Dairyman Crick sent all the dairy people out into a field to search for garlic plants. One bite by one cow was enough to make the whole day's butter taste of garlic. It was not by accident that Clare walked next to Tess.

'Don't they look pretty?' she said to him.

'Who?'

'Izzy Huett and Retty.' She had decided that either would make a good farmer's wife.

'Pretty? Well, yes, I have often thought so.'

'They are excellent dairywomen.'

'Yes, though not better than you.' Clare observed them.

'She is blushing,' continued Tess bravely, 'because you are looking at her.' She could hardly say 'Marry one of them if you really don't want a fine lady! Don't think of marrying me!' From now on she tried to avoid spending time with Angel. She gave the other three every chance.

11

It was July and very hot. The atmosphere of the flat valley hung like a drug over the dairy people, the cows and the trees. It was Sunday morning after milking. Tess and the other three girls dressed quickly to go to Mellstock Church, which was three or four miles away from Talbothays. Heavy thunderstorms had poured down the day before, but today the sun shone brightly and the air was warm and clear. When the girls reached the lowest part of the road to Mellstock, they found it was flooded. In working clothes and boots they would have walked through, but they were wearing Sunday white stockings and thin shoes which they did not want to ruin. The church bell was calling, still a mile away.

Suddenly they saw Angel Clare approaching. He had seen them from far away, and had come to help them, one of them in particular.

'I'll carry you through the water, all of you,' he offered. All four blushed as if they had one heart.

'Now, Marian, put your arms round my shoulders. Hold on!' and Angel walked off with her in his arms. Next was Izz Huett. Her lips were dry with emotion. Angel returned for Retty. While he was picking her up, he glanced at Tess. He could not have said more plainly, 'It will soon be you and I.' There was an understanding between them.

It was now Tess's turn. He picked her up. She was embarrassed to discover her excitement at his nearness.

'Three plain girls to get one beauty,' he whispered.

'They are better women than I,' she said bravely.

'Not to me,' said Angel. She blushed. There was silence. Clare stood still and bent his face to hers.

'Oh Tessy!' he said. Her cheeks were pink and she could not look into his eyes. But he respected her modesty and did nothing more. He walked slowly, however, to make the journey as long as possible, and put her down on dry land. Her friends were looking with round thoughtful eyes at them. He said goodbye and went back by the road.

The four walked on together. Marian broke the silence by saying, 'No, we have no chance against her!' She looked joylessly at Tess.

'What do you mean?' asked Tess.

'He likes you best, the very best! We saw as he brought you over. He'd have kissed you if you had encouraged him, only a little.'

They were no longer cheerful but they were not bitter. They were generous country girls who accept that such things happen. Tess's heart ached. She knew that she loved Angel Clare, perhaps all the more passionately because the others also loved him. And yet that same hungry heart of hers pitied her friends.

'I will never stand in your way!' she cried to them that evening

*Angel Clare stood still and bent his face to hers. 'Oh Tessy,'
he said.*

in the bedroom. 'I don't think he's thinking of marrying, but even if he asked me, I'd refuse him, as I'd refuse any man.'

'Oh why?' they asked.

'I cannot marry! But I don't think he will choose any of you.'

So the girls remained friends. They all shared each other's secret. The air in their bedroom was full of their hopeless passion. There was a flame burning the inside of their hearts out. But because they had no hope, they were not jealous of each other. They had even heard that Angel's family were planning for him to marry a neighbour's daughter. Tess no longer attached any importance to Clare's interest in her. It was a passing summer attraction, nothing more.

The heat grew steadily greater. In this stormy atmosphere even a passing attraction would deepen into love. Everything in nature was ready for love. Clare became gradually more passionately in love with the soft and silent Tess. The fields were dry. Waggons threw up clouds of dust on the road. Cows jumped over gates, chased by flies. Dairyman Crick's sleeves were rolled up from Monday to Saturday, and the milkers milked in the fields for coolness.

On one of these afternoons Tess and Angel were milking near each other. Tess used to rest her head on the cow's body, her eyes fixed on a distant field. The sun shone on the beautiful lines of her face. She did not know that Clare had followed her round and sat watching her. How very lovable her face was to him. He had never seen such beautiful lips and teeth, like roses filled with snow.

Suddenly Clare jumped up, leaving his bucket to be kicked over by the cow, went quickly towards her, and, kneeling down beside her, took her in his arms. Tess let herself relax in his arms in a moment of joyful surprise. He was on the point of kissing that tempting mouth, but stopped himself.

'Forgive me, Tess dear!' he whispered. 'I ought to have asked. I love you, Tess, really!'

Tess tried to free herself and her eyes began to fill with tears.

'Why are you crying, my darling?' he asked.

'Oh I don't know!' she murmured, trying to pull away.

'Well, I've shown my feeling at last, Tess,' he said with a curious sigh, showing that his heart had overcome his reason. 'I do love you dearly and truly. But I shall go no further now. I have surprised you.'

She freed herself and they went on milking. Nobody had noticed, and when Dairyman Crick came round there was no sign to show that there was any connection between them. Yet something had happened which was to change their whole world. As a practical man, the dairyman might laugh at love, but love has a habit of changing people's lives. It is a force to be respected.

The Result

12

The nights were as hot as the days. Angel Clare could not sleep. He went out into the darkness to think over what had happened that afternoon. He had come as a student of farming to this dairy, thinking he would be here only a short time. He thought it would be a quiet place. From here he could observe the great world outside, before **plunging back** into it. But the world outside had lost its interest, and the quiet place was now the centre of all feeling.

Clare was a thoughtful, honest man. He knew Tess was not a toy to play with and throw away when finished with. Her life was as important to her as his was to him. He knew he must treat her affection for him seriously. But if they went on meeting every day, their relationship must develop: he could not stop himself. As he had not decided what purpose their relationship should have, he decided that for the moment they should meet as little as possible. But it was not easy to keep to this decision. He was driven towards her by the heat in his blood.

He thought he would go and see his family. In less than five months he would have finished his studies here. After a few more months on other farms, he would be ready to start farming himself. Shouldn't a farmer's wife be a woman who understood farming?

He rode along the narrow road towards Emminster and his parents' house. His eyes were looking, not at the road, but at next year. He loved her: ought he to marry her? What would his mother and brothers say? What would he himself say two years after the wedding?

As he rode into the village, he saw a group of young girls waiting outside the church. Walking quickly to join them was Miss Mercy Chant, only daughter of his father's neighbour. His parents quietly hoped Angel would marry Mercy one day. She was very good at giving Bible classes, but in Angel's mind was the face of the pretty milkmaid who hardly ever thought of God.

His family were delighted, though surprised, to see him. Angel was glad to be at home, and yet he did not feel so much part of the family as he used to. His father's religious belief was very strict, but he was a kind, honest man, and fond of his sons. However, he would have been shocked to know of the pagan pleasure in nature and pretty womanhood experienced by Angel. His mother shared his father's religious views and helped in his church work. His brothers seemed rather unimaginative and narrow-minded, although they were both well educated: they felt that anybody outside the Church or university could not be respected.

As he walked with his brothers, Angel felt that, however lucky they were to have a university education, neither of them really saw life as it was lived. They thought farming was a poor man's job, not suitable for a gentleman. Angel felt all the more determined to keep to his choice.

In the evening he spoke to his father alone after prayers. Mr Clare told his son he had been saving the money he would have spent on his university education for him. This encouraged Angel to ask his father what sort of wife a farmer needed.

'A really Christian woman. Nothing else matters. For example, my neighbour Dr Chant . . .'

'But isn't the main thing that she should be able to milk cows, churn good butter, value animals and direct farm workers?'

Mr Clare had clearly never thought of this before.

'Yes, yes, certainly. But I was going to say that you will never

find a purer woman than Mercy Chant. Your mother and I
would be very happy if you . . .'

'Yes, yes, Mercy is good, I know. But, father, don't you think
that one who is just as good and pure, and who understands
farm life as well as the farmer, would be much better?'

After much discussion Angel got down to details. He
explained he had met a woman who was ideally suited to be a
farmer's wife, who went to church regularly, who was honest,
sensitive, intelligent, graceful, pure as snow, and extremely
beautiful.

'Is she of a good family, like Mercy?' asked his surprised
mother, who had come in during the conversation.

'She is not what we call a lady,' said Angel firmly. 'She is a
cottager's daughter. What's the advantage of good family to
me? My wife will have to work hard and manage with very little
money.'

'Mercy is educated. That has its charm,' said his mother,
looking at him through her silver glasses.

'I shall help her with her reading. She will learn fast. She's full
of poetry, real poetry. She lives what poets only write. And she is
a good Christian girl. I'm sure you'll value her for that.'

His parents already doubted Angel's religious belief, so they
were almost relieved to hear this of his future wife. They told
him not to act in a hurry, but they would like to see her.
Although Angel was free to marry or not as he wished, he did
not want to hurt his parents, and he accepted their advice.

As he set off to return to the dairy and Tess, his father rode
with him a little way. Mr Clare was telling his son about the
new d'Urberville family who had taken the ancient name and
lived near Trantridge. There was a young man and his blind
mother. Preaching in the church there one day, Mr Clare had
spoken out bravely against the well-known wickedness of young

d'Urberville, who, after this, had publicly insulted him when they met later.

Angel was angry with d'Urberville. 'Dear father, you should not let yourself be insulted like that!'

'It doesn't matter to me. I have a duty to point out where people go wrong. Often men have hit me, but then at least they haven't hit their families. And they live to thank me, and praise God.'

'I hope this young man does the same!' said Angel warmly. 'But it doesn't seem likely.'

'We'll hope anyway,' said Mr Clare. 'Maybe one of my words may grow like a seed in his heart one day.'

Angel could not accept his father's narrow religious beliefs, but he loved him for his courage. He remembered that his father had not once asked whether Tess had money or not. This lack of interest in money meant that all the brothers would probably be poor for ever, but Angel still admired his father's belief that money was not important.

When he returned to the dairy, in the sleepy afternoon heat, nobody was awake. Getting up so early in the morning meant the milkers really needed a sleep before the afternoon milking. It was three o'clock, time for skimming. There was a slight noise upstairs, then Tess appeared before his eyes. She did not see him, and stretched one arm up above her head. She yawned like a cat and he saw the red inside of her mouth. Her whole soul breathed out physical beauty. Then her eyes flashed as she recognized him.

'Oh Mr Clare! How you frightened me – I . . .' she said, looking glad, shy and surprised at the same time.

Clare stepped forward to put his arms round her.

'Dear, darling Tessy!' he whispered, putting his face to her warm cheek. 'Don't call me Mr Clare any more! I've hurried back because of you!'

They stood holding each other, the sun warming them through the window. He looked deep into her eyes of blue and black and grey. She looked at him as Eve must have looked at Adam.

'I must go skimming,' she said. Together they went to the milk-house.

Perhaps the Talbothays milk was not very well skimmed that afternoon. Tess was in a dream as she skimmed. The heat of his love made her feel like a plant under a burning sun.

'There's something very practical that I want to ask you,' he said gently. 'I shall soon want to marry. Being a farmer, I need a wife who knows all about farms. Will you be that woman, Tessy?'

She looked quite worried. She had accepted that she could not help loving him, but she had not expected this result. With bitter pain she replied as she had promised herself she would.

'Oh Mr Clare – I cannot be your wife . . . I cannot be!' The sound of these words seemed to break her very heart.

'But Tess!' he said, amazed at her answer and holding her still closer. 'Surely you love me?'

'Oh yes, yes! And I would rather be yours than anybody's in the whole world! But I *cannot* marry you!' cried the sweet and honest voice miserably.

'Tess, have you agreed to marry someone else?'

'No, no!'

'Then why do you refuse me?'

'Your father is a parson, and your mother will want you to marry a lady,' said poor Tess, desperately trying to find an excuse.

'No, certainly not, that's why I went home, to talk to them both.'

'I feel I cannot – never, never!'

'Is it too sudden, my pretty? I'll give you time. I won't mention it again for a while.'

She tried to skim again, but her tears fell so that she could not do it. She could never explain her sadness, even to this her best friend. Clare began to talk more generally, to calm her. He talked about his father's religious views, and the good work he did. He mentioned the insults his father had received from a young man near Trantridge who had a blind mother.

Tess now looked hard and worn, and her mouth was tragic. Clare did not notice. They finished skimming and he said to her softly:

'And my question, Tessy?'

'Oh no – no!' she replied, hopelessly, thinking bitterly of Alec d'Urberville. 'It *can't* be!'

She went out with the other milkmaids to the cows in the fields. Angel watched her moving freely in the air like a swimmer on a wave. He knew he was right to choose a wife from nature, not from civilization.

13

Clare was not depressed by Tess's refusal, feeling sure that she would finally accept him. A few days later he asked her again.

'Tess, why did you say "no" so positively?'

'I'm not good enough.'

'Not enough of a fine lady?'

'Yes. Your family would not respect me.'

'You know, you're wrong. My father and mother would. And

I don't care about my brothers.' He held her to stop her slipping away. 'You didn't mean it, did you? I can't work or read or play or anything until I know that you will some day be mine! Say you will, Tess!'

She could only shake her head and look away.

'Then I ought not to hold you, to talk to you like this? Why, Tess?'

'It is for your good, my dearest! I can't give myself the great happiness of promising to be yours − because I am *sure* I ought not to!'

'But you will make me happy!'

'Ah, you think so, but you don't know!'

After a struggle like this, Tess would go to the fields or her room to cry. Her heart was so strongly on the side of his that she feared she might give way.

'Why doesn't somebody tell him all about me?' she thought. 'It was only forty miles away. Somebody must know!' But nobody knew and nobody told him.

Tess's life now had two parts, positive pleasure and positive pain. Every time she and Angel were alone together he would ask her again, and she would refuse. She was keeping her promise to herself, but in her heart of hearts Tess knew that eventually she would accept him. Love and nature both advised her to have him without thinking of complications, to delight in passion without considering future pain.

'I know I shall say yes − I can't help it!' she cried to herself in bed one night. 'But it may kill him when he knows! Oh, oh!'

'I've got some news for you all,' said Dairyman Crick as they sat down to breakfast one Sunday morning. 'It's that Jack Dollop again.'

'The lover in the butter-churn?' said Angel Clare, looking up from his newspaper. 'And has he married the young milkmaid, as he promised?'

'Not he, sir,' replied the dairyman. 'He's married an older woman who had £50 a year. They married in a great hurry and then she told him that by marrying she'd lost her £50 a year! He only married her for her money too. So now they're always quarrelling.'

'She ought to have told him just before they went to church,' said Marian.

'She ought to have seen he only wanted her money, and refused him,' said Retty.

'What do you say, my dear?' the dairyman asked Tess.

'I think she ought . . . to have told him the truth — or else refused him . . . I don't know,' replied Tess, who could not swallow her food. She soon left the table and went into the fields, feeling the pain in the story. She had continued to refuse Angel's offers of marriage, but from that Sunday he changed his approach towards her. He looked for her and came to talk to her at every possible moment, at milking, butter-making, cheese-making, among chickens and among pigs. She knew she could not resist much longer. She loved him so passionately, and he was so like a god in her eyes. He treated her as if he would love and defend her under any circumstances. This began to make her feel less afraid about agreeing to marry him, and telling him the truth about herself.

The days were shorter now, and in the mornings the dairy worked by candlelight. One morning between three and four she ran up to Clare's room to wake him, before waking the others. Having dressed, she was about to go downstairs when Angel came out of his room and stopped her.

'Now, miss,' he said firmly. 'You *must* give me an answer or I shall have to leave the house. You aren't safe with me. I saw you just now in your nightdress. Well? Is it yes at last?'

'I really will think seriously about it, Mr Clare.'

'Call me Angel then, and not Mr Clare. Why not Angel dearest?'

'It would mean I agree, wouldn't it?'

'It would only mean you love me, and you did admit that long ago.'

'Very well then, Angel dearest, if I must,' she murmured, smiling. Clare could not resist kissing her warm cheek.

After milking and skimming, all the dairy people went outside. Tess generously tried for the last time to interest Angel in the other dairymaids.

'There's more in those three than you think,' she said. 'Any of them would make you a better wife than I could. And perhaps they love you as much as I do – almost.'

'Oh Tessy!' he cried impatiently. She was so relieved to hear this that she could not make any further self-sacrifice. She knew that this day would decide it.

In the late afternoon Angel Clare offered to drive the waggon with its buckets of milk to the station. He persuaded Tess to go with him.

At first there was silence as they drove along the quiet road, simply enjoying being close to each other. Soon drops of rain started falling. Tess's cheeks were pink and her long hair was wet. She had no jacket, and crept close to Clare. She held an old piece of cloth over them both to keep the rain off.

'Well, dear,' said Angel, 'what about my question?'

'I'll answer you soon.'

'Before we get home?'

'I'll try.'

They passed an old house. Angel explained that it was an interesting place which belonged to the ancient family of the d'Urbervilles.

'It's very sad when a noble family dies out,' he said.

'Yes,' said Tess.

At last they reached the station and watched the milk being lifted on to the train. Tess was fascinated.

'Londoners will drink it for breakfast, won't they? People who don't know we drove for miles in the rain so that it might reach them in time.'

'That's true, but we drove a little for our own reasons too. Now Tess,' he said anxiously, as they drove away into the night, 'your heart belongs to me. Why can't you give me your hand as well?'

'My only reason is you . . . I have something to tell you – I must tell you about my past life!'

'Tell me if you want to, dearest. I expect you have had as many experiences as that flower over there!'

'I grew up in Marlott. And at school they said I would make a good teacher. But there was trouble in my family. Father didn't work very hard and he drank a little.'

'Poor child! That's nothing new.' He held her more closely to his side.

'And there is something unusual about me. I . . . I am not a Durbeyfield, but a d'Urberville. I'm a descendant of the same family who owned that house we passed.'

'A d'Urberville! And is that the whole story, Tess?'

'Yes,' she answered faintly.

'Well, why should I love you less because of that?'

'The dairyman told me you hated old families.'

He laughed. 'Well, I hate the idea that noble blood should be more important than anything else. But I am really very interested in your news. What do *you* think of it?'

'I think it's sad, especially here, to see the fields which once belonged to my ancestors.'

'So that's the awful secret!'

She had not told him. At the last moment she had not been brave enough.

Angel was delighted. 'You see, Tess, society likes a noble name, and will accept you better as my wife, because you are a d'Urberville. Even my mother will like you better. You must use the name of d'Urberville from this very day.'

'I like the other name best.'

'But you *must*! By the way, there's someone who has taken the d'Urberville name near The Chase. Yes, he's the man who insulted my father. How strange!'

'Angel, I would rather not take that name!'

'Now then, Teresa d'Urberville, I've got you! Take my name and you will escape yours!'

'If it is *sure* to make you happy and you do wish to marry me *very* very much . . .'

'I do, dearest, of course! Say you will be mine for ever!'

He held her and kissed her.

'Yes!' No sooner had she said it than she burst into a dry hard sobbing. Angel was surprised.

'Why are you crying?'

'I'm crying because I promised I would die unmarried! Oh, I sometimes wish I had never been born!'

'Tess, how could you wish that if you really loved me? I wish you could prove your love in some way.'

'Will this prove it more?' cried Tess desperately, holding him close and kissing him. For the first time Clare learnt what a passionate woman's kisses were like, on the lips of one she loved with all her heart and soul, as Tess loved him.

'There – now do you believe?' she asked, wiping her eyes.

'Yes. I never really doubted – never!'

They drove on in the darkness, forming one bundle under the cloth.

'I must write to my mother,' she said.

'Of course, dear child. Where does she live?'

'In Marlott.'

'Ah, then I *have* seen you before . . .'

'Yes, when you would not dance with me. Oh, I hope that doesn't mean bad luck!'

After this decision Tess wrote an urgent letter to her mother. This was the reply she received:

Dear Tess,

I hope you are well, as I am. We are all glad to hear you are going to be married soon. But Tess, in answer to your question, whatever you do, *don't* tell your future husband anything about your past experience. No girl would be so foolish, especially as it is so long ago, and not your fault at all. Remember you promised me you would never tell anybody. Best wishes to your young man.

Love from your mother

Tess could not accept her mother's view of life, but perhaps Joan was right in this. Silence seemed best for Angel's happiness. So she grew calm, and from October onwards she was completely happy. Clare seemed the perfect guide, thinker, and friend. She saw perfection in his face, his intelligence, and his soul. She dismissed the past from her mind.

They spent all their time together, as country people do once they are engaged. In the wonderful autumn afternoons they walked by streams, crossing on little wooden bridges. They saw tiny blue fogs in the shadows of trees and hedges, and at the same time bright sunshine in the fields. The sun was so near the ground that the shadows of Clare and Tess stretched a quarter of a mile ahead of them, like two long pointing fingers. When Clare talked to Tess of their future, and the farm they would

*Angel and Tess spent all their time together, as country people
do once they are engaged.*

have abroad, she could hardly believe that she would be going through the world by his side. Her feeling for him was now the breath and life of Tess's being. It made her forget her past sorrows, but she knew they were waiting like wolves for their moment to attack.

One day she cried out to Angel: 'Why didn't you stay and love me when I was sixteen . . . when you danced in Marlott? Oh, why didn't you?'

'Ah yes! If only I had known! But you must not regret so bitterly! Why should you?'

Hiding her feelings quickly, she said, 'I would have had four more years of your love than I can ever have now.'

They had to tell the dairyman and his wife that they were planning to marry. That night as Tess entered the bedroom, all three dairymaids were waiting for her.

'You *are* going to marry him!' said Marian.

'Yes, some day,' said Tess.

'Going to marry *him*, a gentleman!' said Izz.

'It's strange,' said Marian, 'to think Tess will be his wife, not a fine lady, but a girl who lives like us.'

'Do you all hate me for it?' asked Tess in a low voice.

'I want to hate you, but I cannot!' said Retty.

'That's how I feel!' said Marian and Izz.

'He ought to marry one of you,' murmured Tess. 'You are all better than I am!'

'No, no, dear Tess,' they all said.

'I think I ought to make him marry one of you even now!' she sobbed. They went up to her and calmed her and helped her to bed. Before they went to sleep, Marian whispered, 'You will think of us when you are his wife, Tess, and how we did not hate you, because we did not expect to be chosen by him.'

The girls did not know that Tess cried even more at this,

and that she decided she would tell Angel all her history.

Because of this, she would not set a date for the wedding. She wanted to stay as she was, not move forward into a new life. But soon it was clear that the dairyman did not want so many dairymaids at this time of year. Tess would have to leave the dairy at Christmas.

'I'm afraid I'm glad of it,' said Angel to her, 'because now we must decide when to marry. We can't go on like this for ever.'

'I wish we could. I wish it could be always summer and autumn, with you always loving me!'

'I always shall.'

'Oh, I know you will! Angel, I'll fix the day!'

So they decided on 31st December. The wedding was to take place as privately as possible at the dairy. Tess now felt she could not stop things happening, and agreed passively to whatever Angel suggested. In fact Angel's plans were a little hurried. He had not meant to marry so soon. But he wanted to keep her with him, to help her with her reading and studying, so that he could present her proudly as a lady to his parents. He also planned to spend some time studying work in a flour-mill. They could spend their honeymoon staying in the old farmhouse which had once belonged to the d'Urbervilles, while Angel studied at the mill nearby.

The day, the impossible day of their wedding, came closer. His wife, Tess said to herself. Could it ever be?

Angel and Tess decided to spend a day together shopping on Christmas Eve. They went into town in a borrowed carriage. The town was full of strangers, who stared at Tess, happy and beautiful on Angel's arm. At the end of the day, Tess was waiting for Angel to bring the horse and carriage, when two men passed her in the street.

'She's a lovely maiden,' one said to his friend.

'She's lovely, yes. But she's no maiden,' replied the other.

Angel returned at that moment and heard these words. Wildly angry at this insult to Tess, he hit the man in the face. The man said quickly:

'I'm sorry, sir, I must have made a mistake.'

Angel accepted this, gave the man some money, said goodnight, and drove off with Tess. The two men went in the opposite direction.

'And was it a mistake?' asked the second man.

'Certainly not,' said his friend.

On the way home Tess was very serious. She felt she could not tell him the truth to his face, but there was another way. So she went to her room and wrote a four-page letter describing exactly what had happened three or four years ago. In the night she crept up to Angel's room and pushed the letter under his door.

Next morning she looked anxiously at him, but he kissed her as usual. He said nothing about the letter. Had he read it? Did he forgive her? Every morning and night he was the same, until finally the wedding day came.

Tess had not invited her family from Marlott. Angel had written to his. His brothers had not replied, and his parents wrote that they hoped he was not hurrying into marriage, but that he was old enough to decide for himself. Angel did not mind, because he was planning to introduce Tess to them as a d'Urberville as well as a dairymaid, some months later.

Tess was still worried about her confession, and left the crowd of busy people downstairs to creep silently up to Angel's bedroom. There she found her letter unopened, just under the carpet. He had not seen it. She could not let him read it now, in the middle of the preparations. She found him alone for a moment.

'I must confess all my mistakes to you!' she said, trying to keep her words light.

'Not today, my sweet! We'll have plenty of time later on! I'll confess mine too.'

'Then you really don't want me to?'

'I don't, Tessy, really.'

From now on, her one desire, to call him husband, and then if necessary to die, carried her on. She moved in a cloud.

There were few people in the church. At one point she let her shoulder touch Clare's arm, to be sure that he was really there. It was only when she came out that she noticed the carriage they were driving back in. She felt she must have seen it in a dream.

'Oh, maybe you know the story of the d'Urberville carriage,'

There, under the carpet, Tess found her letter unopened.
Angel had not seen it.

said Angel, 'and this one reminds you of it. In the past a certain d'Urberville committed a crime in his carriage, and since then d'Urbervilles see or hear the old carriage whenever . . . But it's rather depressing to talk about.'

'Is it when we are going to die, Angel, or is it when we have committed a crime?'

'Now, Tess!' He kissed her. But she had no energy left. She was now Mrs Angel Clare, but wasn't she really Mrs Alexander d'Urberville?

Later that afternoon they left the dairy. All the dairy people watched them leave, and Clare kissed the dairymaids goodbye. As he was thanking the dairyman, a cock crowed just in front of him.

'That's bad!' whispered the dairymen to each other. 'When a cock crows at a husband like that . . .' and they laughed together behind their hands.

'Go away!' shouted Mr Crick at the cock. Later he said to his wife, 'Why did it have to crow at Mr Clare like that?'

'It only means a change in the weather,' said Mrs Crick, 'not what you think. That's impossible.'

Tess and Angel arrived at the old d'Urberville farmhouse. It was empty, although a woman came to cook and clean for them. They had their tea together, and Clare delighted in eating from the same plate as Tess. Looking at her he thought, 'Do I realize how important I am to this woman? And how I must look after her? I must never forget to think about her feelings!'

It started to rain as it grew dark outside. Finally a man arrived from the dairy with their bags.

'I'm sorry I'm late, sir,' he said, 'but terrible things have been happening at the dairy. You remember the cock crowing? Well, whatever it means, poor little Retty Priddle has tried to drown herself!'

Tess's one desire, to call Angel husband, and then if necessary to die, carried her on.

'What happened?' asked Angel.

'Well, after you left, she and Marian walked from one public house to another, drinking. Retty was found in the river, later on. And Marian was found drunk in a field!'

'And Izz?' asked Tess.

'Izz is at home as usual, but very sad and depressed.'

As the man left, Tess sat sadly by the fire, looking into it. They were simple innocent girls who had not been loved. It was wicked of her to take all the love without paying for it. She would pay: she would tell, there and then.

Angel was sitting beside her, holding her hand. Their faces were red in the firelight.

'This morning,' he said suddenly, 'we said we would both confess our mistakes. I must tell you something and you must forgive me. Perhaps I ought to have told you before. I've put off telling you, because I didn't want to lose you.'

'Angel, I'm sure I'll forgive you . . .' A wild hope was making Tess's heart beat faster.

'Well, wait a minute. You know how much I believe in goodness and purity. But I myself, when I was in London years ago, did wrong with a woman I hardly knew. It lasted two days. I came home and I have never done anything like it since. Do you forgive me?'

'Oh Angel, of course I do! And I am almost glad, because now *you* can forgive *me*! I have a confession too.'

'Ah yes, well confess, you wicked little girl! It can hardly be more serious than mine.'

'It can't, no, it can't!' She jumped up joyfully at the hope. 'No, in fact, it is just the same. I will tell you now.'

She sat down again. They held hands. The fire burned like a Judgement Day fire. Her shadow rose high on the wall. Putting her head against his, she bravely told the whole story of her meeting with Alec d'Urberville and its results.

The Woman Pays

14

H er story came to an end. She had not raised her voice: she had not cried. But things seemed to change as the story progressed. The fire looked as if it was laughing at her troubles. All the objects around her appeared not to care about her tragic history. And yet it was only a short time since he had been kissing her. Everything looked different now.

Clare stirred the fire. It was unnecessary, but he felt he had to do something. He had not really taken in the whole story yet. He stood up. Now as he began to understand the story in its full horror, his face was like an old man's. He made uncertain movements, because everything in his head was vague and uncertain. He could not make himself think clearly.

'Tess! Can I believe this? Are you mad perhaps? My wife, my Tess – you aren't mad, are you?'

'I am not,' she said.

'And yet,' he said, looking strangely at her, 'why didn't you tell me before? Oh yes, you would have told me, in a way, but I stopped you, I remember!'

He was talking but could not think at the same time. His brain seemed to have stopped working. He turned away from her. Tess followed him and stood there staring at him with dry eyes. Then she went down on her knees beside him.

'In the name of our love, forgive me!' she whispered with a dry mouth. 'I have forgiven you for the same!'

And as he did not answer, she said again,

'Forgive me as you are forgiven! *I* forgive *you*, Angel!'

'You – yes, you do.'

'But you do not forgive me?'

'Oh, Tess, it's not a question of forgiveness! You were one person, now you are another. How can forgiveness put that right?'

He paused, considering this. Then suddenly he started laughing in an unnatural, horrible way. It was like a laugh out of hell.

'Don't – don't!' she cried, her face dead white. 'It kills me, that laugh! Angel, do you know what you're doing to me? I've been hoping, longing, praying to make you happy!'

'I know that.'

'I thought, Angel, that you loved me – me, my very self! If you *do* love me, how can you treat me like this? It frightens me! Having begun to love you, I will love you for ever, in all changes, in all troubles, because you are yourself. I ask no more. Then how can you, my husband, stop loving me?'

'I repeat, the woman I have been loving is not you.'

'But who is she?'

'Another woman in your shape.'

Suddenly she realized how he saw her. For him she was a guilty woman pretending to be an innocent one. There was terror in her white face as she saw this. She could not stand, and he stepped forward, thinking she might fall.

'Sit down,' he said gently. 'You are ill, and I am not surprised.'

She sat down, her face still full of fear and her eyes wild.

'I don't belong to you any more then, do I, Angel?' she asked helplessly. And at last the tears came. Clare watched her sobbing, and waited until the first violence of her emotion had passed.

'Angel,' she said suddenly in a normal voice, 'am I too wicked for us to live together?'

'I haven't had time to think what we should do.'

'I won't ask you to let me live with you, Angel, because I have no right to! I won't write to tell my family we are married, as I said I would.'

'Won't you?'

'No, I won't do anything unless you order me to. And if you go away, I won't follow you. And if you never speak to me again, I won't ask why, unless you tell me I can.'

'And if I order you to do anything?'

'I'll obey you, even if I have to lie down and die.'

'How good of you. But it seems you have changed. In the past you were keen to look after yourself. Now you are keen to sacrifice yourself.'

Clare's bitter words, however, were not fully understood by Tess. She only knew that he was angry with her. She stood silent, not knowing that he was struggling with his love for her. She did not observe a large tear rolling slowly down his cheek. He was realizing what a change Tess's confession had made to his whole life. He had to decide on some action.

'Tess,' he said, as gently as he could, 'I can't stay here just now. I'm going out.'

He quietly left the room. Two glasses of wine, ready for their supper, remained untouched on the table. Only two or three hours earlier they had drunk tea from the same cup.

As he closed the door behind him, Tess jumped up. He had gone: she could not stay. She put out the candles and followed him. The rain was over and the night was now clear.

Clare walked slowly and without purpose. His shape was black and frightening. She walked just behind him. There was water on the road, where the stars could be seen reflected. Away from the house the road went through the fields. She followed Clare as a dog follows its owner.

Eventually Tess could not help speaking to him.

'What have I done? *Nothing* interferes with my love for you. You don't think I planned it, Angel, do you? I would not deceive you like that!'

'H'm, well. No, maybe you would not, but you are not the same. No, not the same. But don't make me blame you.'

She went on begging for forgiveness. Perhaps she said things that would have been better left to silence.

'Angel! Angel! I was a child when it happened. I knew nothing of men.'

'I admit it was not so much your fault as his.'

'Then won't you forgive me?'

'I do forgive you, but forgiveness isn't everything.'

'And do you love me?'

He did not answer this question.

'Oh Angel — my mother says she knows several cases which were worse than mine, and the husband has not minded much . . . well, he has accepted it at least. And in those cases the woman hasn't loved him as I love you!'

'Don't, Tess, don't argue. Those are just country people's ways. There is a correct way of doing things. I think that parson who discovered you were a d'Urberville should have kept quiet. Perhaps you were weak and could not refuse this man because your ancient noble blood has run thin, because your family is no good any more. I thought you were a child of nature, but you have the worst of your ancient family in you!'

Tess accepted his bitterness, not understanding the details. He did not love her as he had done, and nothing else mattered.

They went on again in silence. They walked slowly for hours, with sad anxious faces, not talking, one behind the other, like a funeral procession.

Tess said to her husband:

'I don't want to cause you sadness all your life. The river is down there. I can put an end to myself in it. I'm not afraid.'

'Don't talk like that. Do what I ask, go back to the house and go to bed.'

'I will,' she said obediently.

When she returned to the house, she found everything as they had left it and the fire still burning. She went to the bedroom. There was a mistletoe branch hanging above the bed. Now she understood why Angel had brought a strange parcel with him. It was to surprise her. He had delightedly hung it there. Now it looked foolish and out of place.

As she had nothing more to fear, and nothing more to hope for, she lay down. In a few moments lonely Tess was asleep, in the bedroom once used by the young wives of her ancestors.

Later on that night Clare also came back to the house. He prepared a bed downstairs, but crept shoeless upstairs to see if Tess was asleep. He was relieved to see her sleeping deeply. And yet he felt he alone had the whole worry of what action to take, and the responsibility for her life as well as his. He turned away from her door, and then turned back again, pulled by his love for her. But his eye was caught by a painting on the wall of one of Tess's ancestors, a proud fierce woman, who looked as if she hated and wanted to deceive all men. He thought she and Tess looked alike. That was enough to stop him, and he went downstairs to his lonely bed.

He looked calm and cold, full of self-control. His face showed he had fought against passion and won, but did not like being the winner. He still found it difficult to accept that Tess, the pure village maiden, was not what she seemed. How unexpected life could be! He put out the candle. The night came in, unconcerned and uninterested, the night which had swallowed up his happiness.

15

Whn Clare woke up the next morning, the sky was grey
and the sun was not shining. The fireplace in the room
was full of cold ashes. The two full glasses of wine still stood
untouched on the table.

When the cleaning woman came, he sent her away, not
wanting a third person in the house. He found wood to make a
fire, and prepared breakfast. People passing the farmhouse saw
the smoke rising from the chimney, and envied the newly-
married couple in their happiness.

'Breakfast is ready!' he called upstairs in a normal voice.

Tess came down immediately. She was already dressed, but
her hands and face were cold. She had no fire in her bedroom,
where she had been sitting waiting for his call, and staring at the
dying mistletoe. Clare's polite words gave her a moment of
hope, which died, however, when she saw his face.

They were both, in fact, the ashes of their former fires. After
last night's passionate sorrow, they both felt heavy and lacking
in energy.

Tess went up to Angel, touching him lightly with her fingers.
Was this really the man who once loved her? Her eyes were
bright, her cheeks still round, but her lips were pale. She looked
absolutely pure. Angel looked at her in wonder.

'Tess! Say it isn't true! It can't be true!'

'It is true.'

'Every word?'

'Every word.'

He would almost have preferred her to lie, so that he could
believe her blindly, but she repeated, 'It is true.'

'Is he living?' asked Angel.

'The baby died.'

'But the man?'

'He is alive.'

'Is he in England?'

'Yes.'

Despair passed over Clare's face. He moved vaguely around the room.

'Look,' he said, 'I thought – any man would have thought – that if I didn't look for knowledge, good family, and wealth in a wife, if I sacrificed all that, I would be sure of finding a country girl who was at least pure . . . but . . . but I should not accuse you.'

Tess understood his feelings perfectly. She saw that he had lost in every way.

'Angel – I would not have married you if I had not known that, after all, there *is* a way out for you . . . only I hoped you would never . . .' She was close to tears.

'A way out?'

'You can divorce me.'

'Good heavens! How can you be so stupid? How can I divorce you?'

'Can't you, now I have told you everything?'

'Oh Tess, you are so childish! You don't understand the law. No, I can't.'

There was shame and misery in Tess's face.

'I thought you could,' she whispered. 'Don't think I planned this! I really believed you could take that way out. Oh, then I ought to have done it last night. But I didn't have the courage. That's just like me!'

'The courage to do what?' he asked.

'To put an end to myself.'

'Where?'

'In the bedroom, under your mistletoe. With the rope from my box. But I couldn't in the end! I was afraid that people would talk and you would suffer from that.'

Clare was shaken by this unexpected confession.

'Now, listen. You must never think of such a wicked thing again. Promise me as your husband never to do anything like that.'

'I promise. I see it was wicked. But, Angel, it was to set you free, and to avoid a divorce, which everyone would talk about. But dying by my own hand is too good for me. You, my husband, should kill me. I think I would love you more, if that were possible, if you could bring yourself to do it. I am so much in your way!'

'Quiet! Don't talk about it.'

'Well, just as you wish. I will do whatever you like.'

They sat down to breakfast, tired and sad. They did not look at each other and they did not eat much. Angel left soon afterwards to start his studies at the flour-mill nearby. Tess cleared the ashes from the fireplace, cleaned the house and prepared the lunch, waiting for his return. At lunch they talked politely of work at the flour-mill and methods of milling. In the afternoon he went back to the mill, and in the evening he studied his books and papers. Tess felt she was in his way and went to the kitchen. He came to find her there.

'Don't work in the kitchen like this,' he said. 'You're not my servant, you're my wife.'

She looked happier. 'You mean, I can think of myself as that?' she asked, trembling.

'What do you mean, Tess? You *are* my wife, of course.'

'I don't know,' she said, with tears in her eyes. 'I told you long ago I wasn't good enough for you. And I'm not good enough! I was right! But you persuaded me!'

She turned her back on him, sobbing as if her heart would break. It would have won round any man but Angel Clare. Deep in him lay a hard logic, which had resisted the Church, and now resisted Tess. She accepted his treatment of her as being what she deserved. She would never have thought of criticizing his hardness. To her he was still perfection.

Another day passed by in the same way. Only once did Tess try to get closer to her husband. As he was leaving for the flour-mill, she put up her mouth to be kissed. He ignored the invitation, and said goodbye coldly. She felt as if he had hit her. How often had he wanted to kiss her in those happy days at Talbothays!

But on his way to the mill Angel regretted his coldness. He wished he had been kinder to her and kissed her once at least.

So they lived through another day – together in the same house, but more separately than ever before. Clare was desperately wondering what to do. Tess no longer even hoped for forgiveness. That evening she said bravely:

'I suppose you aren't going to live with me long, are you, Angel?' She found it difficult to control the muscles of her face.

'No. How can we live together as man and wife while that man lives? He is your natural husband, I'm not. If he were dead, that might be different. Anyway, have you thought of the future? Have you thought we might have children? They would find out about this. Everybody would talk about it. Can you imagine them growing up under a cloud like that? They would hate you for it.'

Tess's head was bent. Her eyes felt so heavy they were almost closed. 'No, I can't ask you to stay with me,' she whispered. 'I hadn't thought of it like that.'

She had hoped, as women do, that living together for a time would break down his coldness. Being near him every day was her only hope of winning him back. But she had never imagined she might have children who would reject her. She now remembered how she had criticized her mother for bringing babies into the world without being able to look after them. She realized that she might have made the same mistake as Joan Durbeyfield. She completely accepted Angel's argument.

She could have argued that if they went as planned to farm in another country, nobody would know about her past. But perhaps she was right not to argue. A woman knows not only her own sorrow but also her husband's. He might keep the bitterness alive in his heart, even if nobody knew or talked about it at all. She had lost.

On the third day she said, 'I accept what you say. We must separate.'

'But what can you do?'

'I can go home.'

Clare had not thought of that. 'Can you really?'

'Yes. If I am with you all the time, I may persuade you to stay, against your better judgement. Then you and I would both be sorry. I must go.'

'Right,' said Angel. His face was pale but his voice was determined.

Tess was slightly shocked. He had agreed so quickly to her generous offer!

'I didn't like to suggest it,' he said, 'but as *you* have, I think it's a good idea to part – at least for a while. God knows, we may come together again one day!'

So they both prepared to leave the following day. That night Tess was woken by a noise in the house. At first she thought Angel was coming to her bedroom, and her heart beat wildly with joy. But then she saw his eyes staring emptily ahead of him, and knew he was walking in his sleep. He came to the middle of .

her room and said very sadly, 'Dead! Dead! Dead! Poor darling Tess! So sweet, so good, so pure! My wife, dead!'

These words, which he would never say when awake, were very sweet to Tess. She would not have moved to save her life. She lay in absolute stillness, trying not to breathe, wondering what he was going to do with her. Her trust in him was complete.

He picked her up and carried her to the stairs. Was he going to throw her down? She knew he was leaving her the next day, perhaps for ever. She almost hoped they would fall and die together.

He continued downstairs, taking her out of the house towards the river. She had given herself totally up to him, and did not care what happened to her as long as she was with him. They arrived at a place where the river was fast and deep, and Angel started to cross it on the narrow footbridge, still holding Tess. Perhaps he wanted to drown her. Even that would be better than separation.

As they crossed, the water rushed fiercely below them. If Tess had moved in his arms, they would both have fallen into the dangerous water. But she had no right to take his life, although her own was worthless, so she stayed still.

Angel walked purposefully towards a ruined church near the river. Against the old wall was an empty stone tomb. In this he carefully laid Tess, and kissing her lips, sighed deeply and happily. He immediately lay down on the ground next to the tomb, and looked fast asleep.

Tess stepped out of the tomb and managed to persuade Angel to walk back to the house, without waking him. It was very cold outside, and both had only night clothes on. She helped him to his sofa bed in the living room, and he still did not wake up.

Next morning he seemed to remember nothing of the night's experiences, and Tess did not refer to his sleepwalking. They finished packing and left the farmhouse, where they had hoped to be so happy. After driving some distance Angel stopped the carriage to get down and continue on foot. Tess was going further on in the carriage. He spoke seriously to her as they separated.

'Now remember,' he said, 'I am not angry with you, but I cannot bear to live with you at the moment. I will try to accept it. But until I come to you, you should not try to come to me.'

The punishment seemed a heavy one to Tess. Had she really deserved this?

'May I write to you?'

'Oh yes, if you are ill or need anything. You probably won't, so I might be the first to write.'

'I agree to the conditions, Angel, because you know best. Only don't make it too much for me to bear!'

That was all she said. If she had sobbed or fainted or begged him, he would probably have given way. But she made it easy for him. He gave her some money and they said goodbye. He stood on the road watching the carriage continue up the hill, secretly hoping that Tess would look back. But she was lying half dead with misery inside. He turned to walk on alone, not realizing that he still loved her.

16

As the carriage drove on through Blackmoor Vale, Tess now began to awake from her sorrow and wonder how she could face her parents. She left the carriage and came into Marlott on foot. When she entered the little cottage, her mother was doing the washing as usual.

'Why Tess!' she cried when she saw her daughter. 'I thought you were married! Really married this time!'

'Yes, mother, I am.'

'Then where's your husband?'

'Gone away for a time.'

'Gone away! When were you married then? Tuesday, as you said?'

'Yes, mother.'

'Married on Tuesday and today it's only Saturday, and he's gone away! What strange husbands you seem to find, Tess!'

'Mother!' Tess ran across to Joan and put her head on Joan's shoulder. 'You told me I mustn't tell him. But I did – I couldn't help it – and he went away!'

'Oh you fool, you little fool!' cried her mother.

'I know, I know,' sobbed Tess. 'But he was so good! I couldn't lie to him. And if only you knew how much I loved him and how much I wanted to marry him!'

'Well, it's too late now,' said Mrs Durbeyfield. 'Whatever will your father say? He was very proud of your marriage. He's been telling them at the public house that you'll help his noble family become great again. Oh, there he is now!'

Tess ran upstairs, but through the thin walls she could hear the whole story being told to Sir John.

'People will laugh at me in the village!' he said. 'Do you think he really did marry her, Joan? Or is it like the first?'

Tess could listen no more. Even her own family did not believe her. She could not stay. She gave her mother half the money which Clare had given her, and told her family she was going to join him. And so she left Marlott again, looking for work.

Angel Clare also returned home. He had spent three weeks since his wedding trying to remain calm and continue his studies, but with the disturbing picture of Tess always in his mind. He was beginning to wonder if he had treated her unfairly. She had been so much a part of his plans for the future that he was now thinking of countries where they could farm together. The idea of Brazil attracted him. The countryside, people and habits would be so different. Perhaps they could make a new life there together. So he went back to Emminster to tell his parents his new plan.

'But where's your wife, dear Angel?' cried his mother when he arrived.

'She's at her mother's for the moment. I've come home in rather a hurry, because I've decided to go to Brazil.'

'Brazil! But they're all Roman Catholics there!'

'Are they? I hadn't thought of that.'

But Mr and Mrs Clare were even more interested in their son's marriage than in Brazil's religion.

'Angel, we do want to meet your wife. We are not in the least angry about this rather hurried wedding, so why haven't you brought her? It seems strange.'

Angel explained that she would be staying at her mother's while he went to Brazil alone to see if the country was suitable. He planned to bring her to meet his parents before he went there a second time, with her. But his mother was disappointed at not seeing Tess. She watched her son as he ate, and asked questions.

'Is she very pretty?'

'She certainly is!'

'And a maiden of course?'

'Of course.'

'I imagine you were her first love?'

'Exactly.'

His father asked no questions, but when the moment for evening prayers arrived, he chose a passage from the Bible.

'This passage is very suitable, as you are here, Angel. It is in praise of a pure wife.'

'We shall all think of her as your father reads it,' added his mother. As they listened to the ancient, beautiful words, Angel felt like crying.

His mother said, 'You see, Angel, the perfect woman, the Bible tells us, is a working woman, not a fine lady, a girl just like your wife. A girl who uses her hands and heart and head for others. I wish I could have met her, Angel. As she is pure, she is fine enough for me.'

Clare's eyes were full of tears. He quickly said goodnight and went to his room. His mother followed and stood at his door looking anxiously at him.

'Angel, why are you going away so soon? Have you quarrelled with your wife in these three weeks? Angel, is she . . . is she a woman with a past?' The mother's instinct had found the cause of her son's worries.

'She is totally pure!' he replied, and felt that he had to tell that lie, even if he went to hell there and then for it.

'Then never mind the rest. There are few better things in nature than a pure country girl.'

Clare felt furious with Tess, because she had forced him to deceive his parents. Then he remembered her sweet voice, and the touch of her fingers on his face, and her warm breath on his lips. But this well-meaning young man, despite his advanced ideas, was still limited in his thinking. He could not see that Tess was in character as pure as the pure wife in the Bible.

The next day Clare left Emminster and began to prepare for his journey to Brazil. One day, returning from doing some business with a farmer, he happened to meet one of the dairymaids from Talbothays, Izz Huett. He knew her secret: she was an honest girl who loved him and who might have made as good a farmer's wife as Tess. He learnt from Izz that, of the other dairymaids, Retty had become ill, and Marian had started drinking. And Izz herself?

'Suppose I had asked you to marry me, Izz?' he asked.

'I would have said "yes", and you would have had a woman who loved you!'

A wild anger took hold of Clare. Society and its rules had trapped him in a corner. Why shouldn't he take his revenge on society?

'I'm going to Brazil, Izz, without Tess. We have separated for personal reasons. I may never be able to love you, but will you come with me?'

'Yes, I will,' said Izz after a pause.

'You know it's wrong in the eyes of the world, don't you? Do you love me very much? More than Tess?'

'I do, yes, oh, I do love you, but not more than Tess. Nobody could! She would have laid down her life for you.'

Clare was silent. A sob rose inside him. He heard Izz's words again and again in his head: *She would have laid down her life for you.*

'I'm sorry, Izz,' he said suddenly. 'Please forget what I said just now! I must be mad!'

'Oh please take me! Oh, I shouldn't have been so honest!' sobbed Izz.

'Izz, by your honesty you have saved me from doing something wicked. Thank you for that. And please forgive me!'

And so Angel said goodbye to the miserable girl. But he did not turn towards Tess's village. He continued with his plan, and five days later left the country for Brazil.

And so the months passed. Tess found occasional dairy work

for the spring and summer. She sent all Angel's money to her family, who as usual had many expenses and hardly any income. She was too proud to ask Angel's family for more money. That winter she went to work at another farm, where Marian was working. Here the earth was poor, and the work was difficult. But Tess did not mind the hard work in the fields. As she and Marian dug out the vegetables in the pouring rain, they talked of Talbothays and of the sunny green fields and of Angel Clare. Tess did not tell Marian everything, so Marian could not understand why the couple were apart.

They wrote to Izz, asking her to join them if she had no other work. It was the coldest winter for years, but Tess and Marian had to go on working in the snow. Tess realized that the farmer was the same Trantridge man who had recognized her in the market town, and had been knocked down by Angel. He made her work twice as hard as the others.

When Izz came, Tess saw her whispering to Marian. Tess had a feeling it was important. 'Is it about my husband?' she asked Marian later.

'Well yes, Izz said I shouldn't tell. But he asked her to run away to Brazil with him!'

Tess's face went as white as the snow on the ground.

'What happened?'

'He changed his mind. But he was going to take her!'

Tess burst out crying. 'I must write to him! It's my fault! I shouldn't have left it to him! He said I could write to him! I've been neglecting him!'

But in the evening, in her room, she could not finish her letter to him. She looked at her wedding ring, which she wore round her neck in the day, and kept on her finger all night. What kind of husband would ask Izz to go to Brazil with him so soon after parting from his wife?

But this new information made her think again of visiting Angel's family in Emminster. She wanted to know why he had not written to her. She could meet his parents, who would surely be kind to her in her loneliness. So she decided to walk there from the farm at Flintcomb-Ash on a Sunday, her only free day. It was fifteen miles each way. She dressed in her best, encouraged by Marian and Izz, who sent her on her way at four o'clock in the morning. The girls sincerely loved Tess and wished for her happiness. It was a year since her wedding, and on that bright cold morning her unspoken hope was to win over her husband's family and so persuade him back to her.

Although she started cheerfully, she began to lose her courage as she approached Emminster. The church looked forbidding. Perhaps the rather strict parson would not approve of her travelling so far on a Sunday. But she had to go on. She took off her thick walking boots and hid them behind a tree, changing into her pretty shoes. She would collect the boots on the way out of town.

She took a deep breath and rang the bell at the parson's house. Nobody answered. She tried again. Silence. It was almost with relief that she turned and walked away. Then she suddenly remembered that they must all be at church. So she waited in a quiet part of the street until people began to stream out of church. She immediately recognized Angel's brothers and even overheard some of their conversation.

'Poor Angel!' one of them said. 'There's that nice girl, Mercy Chant. Why on earth didn't he marry her instead of rushing into marriage with a dairymaid?'

'It's certainly very strange. But his ideas have always been most odd.'

They joined Mercy Chant as she came out of church, and walked together along the road Tess had walked into Emminster.

'Look, here's a pair of old boots,' said one of the brothers, noticing Tess's boots behind the tree.

'Excellent walking boots, I see,' said Miss Chant. 'How wicked to throw them away! Give them to me. I'll find a poor person who would like them.'

Tess walked quickly past them, tears running down her face. She continued walking as fast as she could away from Emminster. How unlucky that she had met the sons and not the father! Angel's parents would have taken poor lonely Tess to their hearts immediately, as they did every other lost soul, without thought of family or education or wealth.

She grew more and more tired and depressed as she walked the fifteen miles back to Flintcomb-Ash, where only hard work awaited her. But on the way she noticed a crowd listening to a preacher and she stopped for a while to join them. The preacher was describing with enthusiasm how he had been wicked for years and how a certain parson had pointed it out to him: this had gradually turned him from wickedness. But Tess was more shocked by the voice than the words. She moved round behind the crowd to look at his face. As the afternoon sun shone full on him, she recognized Alec d'Urberville.

A Changed Man

17

This was the first time she had seen or heard of d'Urberville since she had left Trantridge. And although he stood there openly as a preacher, as a religious man, she still felt afraid of him. He had changed his clothes, his hair, his moustache and his expression, but could she really believe that he had changed his most secret thoughts and beliefs?

As soon as she recovered from her surprise, she moved away so that he would not notice her. But he suddenly caught sight of her, and the effect on him was electric. His enthusiasm faded, his voice hesitated, his lips trembled, his eyes dropped in confusion. Tess walked rapidly away along the road.

However, as she walked she felt he must be looking at her back as she walked away. And now she knew she could never escape the past, as she had hoped. Reminders of her past would surround her until she died. As she walked uphill she heard footsteps behind her, and, turning, saw that it was the one person in the whole world she did not want to meet this side of the grave.

'Tess!' he said. 'I'm Alec d'Urberville!'

'I see you are,' she said coldly. They walked on together.

'You may wonder why I'm following you. Well, I feel you are the person I would most like to save from hell. So I have come to do that.'

'Have you saved yourself?' Tess asked bitterly.

'God has done it all, not me! I must tell you how I came to believe in Him. Have you ever heard of the parson of Emminster, old Mr Clare? A very strict, sincere man.'

'I have,' said Tess.

'Well, he came to Trantridge once and tried to show me how wicked my life was. I insulted him at the time. But later my mother died, and somehow I began to think about what old Mr Clare said. Since then my one desire has been to help others to understand God too . . .'

'Don't go on!' cried Tess. 'I can't believe in such a sudden change! I almost hate you for talking to me like this, when you know how you've ruined my life! You enjoy yourself for a while and then you make sure of your place in heaven!' As she spoke she looked him full in the face with her great beautiful eyes.

'Don't look at me like that!' said Alec. 'Your eyes remind me of – well, women's faces have too much power over me. Don't look at me! It might be dangerous for you!'

Eventually they came to a crossroads, where a strange stone stood. It was a lonely, unfriendly place, where people did not like to stay for long. Alec stopped here.

'I must go to the right here. I'm preaching at six this evening. Tell me, how has your life been since we last met?'

Tess told him about the baby. Alec was shocked.

'You should have told me! But before we part, come, put your hand on this stone. It was once a holy cross. I'm afraid of your power over me. Swear on the cross that you will never tempt me into wickedness!'

'Good God! How can you ask such an unnecessary thing! I don't want to see you ever again!'

'No, but swear it.'

Tess placed her hand on the stone and swore.

'I shall pray for you,' called Alec as he walked away. 'Who knows, we may meet again!'

Tess went on her way, feeling upset, and soon met a man on the road. He told her that the cross was not religious, but marked the place where a criminal was put to death and buried. Trembling a little at this information, she finally arrived at Flintcomb-Ash.

One day the following week when Tess was working in the fields as usual, Alec d'Urberville came to see her. He explained to her that he intended to sell his land at Trantridge and go to help poor people in Africa.

'Will you help me put right the wicked thing I did to you? Will you be my wife?'

'Oh no, sir!' she cried, horrified.

'Why not?' Disappointment was visible in his face. It was not only duty which pushed him to make this offer, but also his old passion for her.

'You know I don't love you,' answered Tess. 'In fact, I love somebody else.'

'Perhaps that is only a passing feeling . . .'

'No!'

'Yes! Why not? You must tell me!'

'Well, then . . . I have married him.'

'Ah!' he cried and looked hard at her.

'It's a secret here,' she begged. 'Please don't tell anybody.'

'Who is he?' asked d'Urberville. 'Where is he? Why isn't he here to look after you? What sort of husband can he be, leaving you to work like this?'

'Don't ask!' cried Tess, her eyes flashing.

'Your eyes!' whispered Alec. 'I thought I no longer felt anything for you, but when I look into your eyes . . .' He took her hand.

She pulled it quickly away.

'Go now, please, in the name of your new religion, go! Respect me and my husband!'

'Don't worry, I can control myself. I just hoped that our

marriage would take away the bad in both of us. But that plan is no good now.' He walked slowly away, his head bent in thought.

The farmer approached at that moment and was angry with Tess for wasting time talking to a stranger. Tess preferred hard words from this man of stone to sweet ones from Alec d'Urberville. For a moment, however, she imagined escaping from her present hard life by marrying Alec, but rejected it immediately.

At home that night she began a letter to Clare, telling him of her great love for him. Reading between the lines he would have seen her secret fear for the future. But again she could not finish the letter, thinking of his offer to Izz, and so he never received it.

On a Sunday in February she was eating her lunch in the cottage where she lived, when d'Urberville knocked at the door. He rushed in and threw himself into a chair.

'Tess!' he cried desperately. 'I can't help it! I can't stop thinking of you! Pray for me, Tess!'

Tess did not pity him. 'I cannot because I don't believe God would change His plans just because I asked Him.'

'Who told you that?'

'My husband.'

'Ah, your dear husband . . . Tell me what he believes.'

Tess explained, as clearly as she could remember, Angel's beliefs. Alec watched her closely.

'The fact is, you just believe whatever he says. That's just like you women!'

'Ah, that's because he knows everything!' Tess replied with enthusiasm. 'What is good enough for him is good enough for me.'

'H'm, interesting,' murmured d'Urberville. 'Perhaps he understands religion better than old Mr Clare. Perhaps he's right not to attach too much importance to the Bible and to fixed ideas. Perhaps I was wrong to become a preacher. Today I should be preaching at half-past two, and here I am! My passion for you was too strong for me!'

'You have let all those people down? They are waiting for you!'

'What do I care? You are the one woman I have always wanted. Why have you tempted me away from religion? I can't resist you!' His black eyes flashed passionately. He advanced towards her.

'I couldn't help your seeing me again!' cried Tess, moving nervously away from him. 'Please leave me! Remember I am married! Remember I can't defend myself!'

Alec stopped, turned, and went out without another word. But he went on thinking of Angel's religious logic, as explained by Tess. It seemed to make sense. 'That clever husband doesn't know that his ideas may lead me back to her!' he laughed to himself.

In March the threshing-machine came for a day to Flintcomb-Ash. It was a huge red machine which ate all the corn the farm-workers could feed it. Next to it stood the engine which ran it, and the engineer. He lived in a world of fire and smoke, and was permanently black, as if he came from hell. The farmer put Tess next to the threshing-machine, so that she had the hardest and most tiring job of all. She had little chance to talk or rest, and at lunch time was about to start eating when she noticed d'Urberville approaching. He had changed his parson's clothes and now looked just like the young gentleman she had first met at Trantridge.

'I am here again, you see,' he said, smiling at her.

'Why do you bother me like this?' she cried.

'*You* trouble *me*! Your eyes look at me night and day. I can't forget them. Tess, when you told me about that child of ours, my feelings for you became strong again. I have lost interest in religion and it is your fault!'

'You have stopped preaching?' asked Tess, shocked.

'I have. What a lot of stupid people they are to listen to a preacher anyway! And I am convinced that your wonderful husband's views are better than old Parson Clare's. I don't know how I became so enthusiastic! So now, here I am, my love, just as in the old times!'

'Not like that at all, no, now it's different!' she said firmly. 'Oh why couldn't you stay religious?'

'Because you've explained your husband's ideas so well to me that I accept them! Ha ha! But seriously, Tess, you need help. I am here and this husband of yours is not. Come with me! My carriage is waiting the other side of the field! You have tempted me, now share my life for ever!' He put an arm round her waist. Tess was red with anger but said nothing. She picked up a heavy leather glove and hit him in the face with it. It was an action which her ancestors must have often practised. Alec jumped up and wiped the blood from his mouth.

'Remember one thing!' he said angrily, only just controlling himself as he held her by the shoulders. 'Remember, my lady, if you are any man's wife, you are mine! I will have you again! I'll come back for an answer later on!'

So he left, and the farm-workers started the afternoon's threshing. It went on until the evening, as the work had to be finished that day. Tess became more and more exhausted and was near to fainting when they finally stopped. Alec d'Urberville, who had been waiting for this moment, appeared at her side.

'You are so weak,' he said, holding her arm. 'I've told the farmer he should not use women for work with the threshing-machine. It's too hard. I'll walk home with you.'

'Oh yes, please do!' murmured Tess, too tired to be afraid of him. 'You are kind sometimes. And at least you wanted to put right the wrong by offering to marry me.'

'If I can't marry you, at least I can help you. I have finished with religion. But you must trust me! I have enough money to help your family and make them comfortable.'

'Have you seen them lately?' asked Tess quickly. 'God knows they need help . . . but no – no, I can take nothing from you, either for them or for me! Please leave me alone!'

As soon as she reached her room she wrote a passionate letter to Angel.

'Remember, my lady, if you are any man's wife, you are mine!
I will have you again!' said d'Urberville angrily.

My own husband,

I must call you that. I must ask you for help – I have no one else! I am so open to temptation, Angel! I cannot tell you who it is. Can't you come to me now, before anything terrible happens? I know you are far away, but I need help! I know I deserved the punishment you gave me, but please, Angel, please be kind to me! If you would come, I could die in your arms!

I live only for you. Don't think I shall be bitter because you left me. I am so lonely without you, my darling!

Haven't you ever felt one little bit of your love for me at the dairy? I am the same woman you fell in love with then, the very same. As soon as I met you, the past was dead for me. Can't you see this?

How silly I was to trust that you would always love me! I ought to have known I couldn't be so lucky.

People say I am still rather pretty, Angel. But I don't care about my looks because you are not here.

If you won't come to me, could I come to you? I'm so worried! I'm afraid I may fall into some wicked trap. Save me from what threatens me!

> Your faithful heartbroken
> Tess

18

This desperate cry for help eventually arrived at the parson's house in Emminster. Old Mr Clare was pleased.

'I think this letter is from Angel's wife. I hope this will bring him home more quickly. He did say he was planning to come home next month.'

'Dear boy, I hope he will get home safely,' murmured Mrs Clare. 'I still feel he should have gone to university like the other two. He should have had the same chance as them, Church or no Church.'

This was the only complaint she ever made to her husband. He too was worried that he had been unfair to Angel. They blamed themselves for this unfortunate marriage. If Angel had studied at Cambridge he would never have become a farmer and married a country girl. Still, his more recent letters showed that Angel was planning to come home to fetch her, so perhaps their quarrel, whatever it was, could be settled.

Angel himself was at this moment riding across Brazil towards the coast. He had never completely recovered from the serious illness he had had when he first arrived. He was not as strong as before, and looked much older. The country had been a disappointment to him. Many farmers had come here from England hoping to make their fortune, and had died in the fields or on the roads. He knew now he could not farm here.

His attitude to life had changed during this time. He began to look again at what was right and wrong. He began to see that a person should be judged not only on what he has done but also on what he wanted to do. He began to think that he had perhaps been unfair to Tess, and he thought about her with growing affection.

He wondered why she had not written. He forgot that he had told her not to write first. He did not realize that she was obeying his orders exactly, although it was breaking her heart.

On his journey, he travelled with another Englishman. They were both depressed and both told each other their problems. The stranger was older and more experienced than Angel. He had a different, more open approach to life. He told Angel clearly that he was wrong in parting from Tess.

The next day they got wet in a thunderstorm. The stranger fell ill and died a few days later. Death came as no surprise in that unfriendly land. Clare buried him, and continued his journey. The man's words were somehow given greater importance by his unexpected death, and suddenly Clare felt ashamed. Tess had committed no crime. He should believe in her character, and not object to a past action she could not avoid. He remembered the words of Izz Huett: *She would have laid down her life for you.* No woman could do more. How she had looked at him on their wedding day – as if he were a god! And during that terrible evening by the fireside, when she told him her story, how desperately sad she had been to realize he might not love her any more.

Meanwhile Tess was not hopeful that Angel would come in answer to her letter. The past had not changed, so he might not change either. Nevertheless she spent her spare time preparing for his possible return, practising singing the songs he used to like, tears rolling down her cheeks all the while.

One evening she was in the cottage as usual when there was a knock at the door. A tall thin girl came in and Tess recognized her young sister Liza-Lu.

'Liza-Lu!' said Tess. 'What's the matter?'

'Mother is very ill,' her sister said seriously, 'and father is not well either and says a man of such noble family shouldn't have to work. So we don't know what to do.'

Tess thought for a moment. She realized she had to go home immediately, although her time was not yet up at the farm. She left her sister to rest for a while, and she herself set off at once with her possessions in a basket.

Although it was night and she had a fifteen-mile walk, she felt quite safe. She was only worried about her mother, and did not notice the strange shapes of trees and hedges in the darkness. At three in the morning she passed the field where she had first seen Angel Clare, and felt again the disappointment when he did not dance with her. And when she saw the family cottage, it seemed to be part of her body and life, as it always did.

She found her mother recovering from her illness, and took over as head of the household. Her father did not seem ill, and had a new plan for earning money.

'I'm going to find all the historians round here,' he said, 'and get them to pay money to keep me going. After all, they pay to look after old ruins, and I'm of historical interest. I think they'll be pleased to do it!'

Tess did not have time to answer. She nursed her mother, fed the children, and worked in the garden, planting vegetables for next year. She enjoyed working outside, among her neighbours. One evening when it was almost dark, she was digging happily in the vegetable garden, some distance from the cottage. It was a clear, fresh night, with smoke blowing about from small fires in the gardens. Suddenly she saw a man's face in the light of a fire. It was d'Urberville! She gasped and stepped back, her face pale.

'What are you doing here?'

'My dear Tess, I just want to help you, to see you. Have you finished at that farm?'

'Yes, I have.'

'Where are you going next? To join your dear husband?'

'Oh, I don't know!' she said bitterly. 'I have no husband!'

'That is quite true in one way. But you have a true friend. When you go back to your cottage, you'll see what I've done for you.'

'Oh Alec, I wish you wouldn't give me *anything*! I – I have enough, I – I just don't want to live at all!' Her tears fell as she started digging again. When she looked round, d'Urberville had left.

On her way back one of her sisters rushed towards her shouting, 'Tess! Tess! Mother is much better but father is dead!'

'But father was only a little bit ill!' said Tess, trying to take in the news.

'He dropped down just now, and the doctor said there was no hope for him because it's his heart!'

Poor John Durbeyfield's death had more importance than his family realized at first. The cottage was in his name. On his death the farmer who owned it decided to put farm workers in it, and told the Durbeyfields to leave. They were not much respected in the village because of John's laziness. Tess also felt guilty that her presence might have influenced the farmer. The village people clearly thought she was not a good example for their children.

So on Lady Day the Durbeyfields had to leave their old home. The night before they left, d'Urberville came to visit Tess, to offer her and her family a little house on his land at Trantridge. Her mother could look after the chickens, and he would pay for the children to go to school. Tess firmly rejected his offer. But when he had gone, for the first time a feeling of anger rose in her against her husband. She had never intended to do wrong and he had punished her too hard! She passionately wrote these few words to him:

Oh why have you treated me so badly, Angel? I do not deserve it. You are cruel! I intend to forget you. You have been so unfair to me!

T

She ran out and posted it before she could change her mind.

'I see there's been a visitor,' said her mother, coming into the living room later. 'Your husband, was it?'

'No, it wasn't him. He'll never, never come,' said Tess hopelessly. She had said it was not her husband, but she was feeling more and more that d'Urberville was physically her husband.

Next day their possessions were put on a waggon and taken to Kingsbere. Mrs Durbeyfield had booked rooms there, as it was the family home of the d'Urbervilles, and she still hoped some good would come of belonging to the ancient family. But as they approached Kingsbere after a long and tiring day's journey, a man came to tell them there were no rooms available. Tess and her mother unloaded the waggon, and left the children and furniture near the churchyard wall, while they looked for somewhere to stay. But all the rooms were full.

Tess looked desperately at the pile of their possessions. In the cold sunlight of this spring evening the furniture looked old and the pots looked worn.

'Tombs belong to families for ever, don't they?' asked her mother brightly, having looked round the churchyard. 'Well, that's where we'll stay, children, until the place of your ancestors finds us some shelter!'

Tess helped her mother move the big bed against the church wall. Underground were the tombs of the d'Urbervilles, and at the head of the bed was a beautiful old window, in which the symbols on the Durbeyfield seal and spoon could be seen. The children were put to bed all together for warmth and comfort.

'Tomorrow we'll find somewhere better!' said Joan cheerfully. 'But Tess, what's the good of you playing at marrying gentlemen, if it leaves us like this!'

Tess went inside the ancient church and stared sadly at the tombs of her ancestors. She thought she saw a movement and turned to look again at a stone figure lying on a tomb. When she saw it was Alec d'Urberville lying there, she almost fainted.

'I'm going to help you,' he said, jumping up and smiling at her. 'You'll see that I'm more useful than a real d'Urberville. I'll see your mother. You'll thank me for this!' As he brushed past her, she dropped her head on to the cold stone of the tomb.

'Why am I on the wrong side of this stone?' she whispered.

Marian and Izz had seen Tess moving house with her family, and knew what a difficult position she was in. They generously hoped she would one day be happy with Angel again, and were afraid for her, knowing that Alec d'Urberville was constantly tempting her. They decided to write a letter to Angel Clare, to inform him of the dangerous situation his wife was in. This is what they wrote:

Dear Sir,

Watch out for your wife if you love her as much as she loves you. She is in danger from an enemy in the shape of a friend. A woman's strength cannot last for ever, and water, if it drops continually, will wear away a stone — yes, even a diamond.

From two well-wishers

The End

19

It was evening in the parson's house at Emminster. Mr and Mrs Clare were waiting anxiously for Angel's return.

'He won't be here yet, my dear,' said old Mr Clare, as his wife went to the front door for the tenth time. 'Remember his train doesn't come in till six o'clock, and then he has to ride ten miles on our old horse.'

'But he used to do it in an hour,' said his wife impatiently. Both knew it was useless to talk about it, and the only thing to do was wait.

When they heard footsteps they rushed outside to meet the shape in the darkness.

'Oh my boy, my boy, home at last!' cried Mrs Clare, who at that moment cared no more for Angel's lack of religion than for the dust on his clothes. What woman, in fact, however firm her beliefs, would not sacrifice her religion for her children? Nothing was more important to Mrs Clare than Angel's happiness.

But as soon as they reached the living room, she saw his face clearly in the light of the candles. She gave a cry and turned away in sorrow. 'Oh, it's not the Angel who went away!'

Even his father was shocked to see the change in his son. They would not have recognized him if they had passed him in the street. The cruel climate and hard work had aged him by twenty years. He was like a shadow, thin and bony, with no spring in his step and no enthusiasm in his eyes.

'I was ill over there,' he said, noticing his parents' concern. He had to sit down, being weak after his journey.

'Has any letter come for me?' he asked eagerly. 'The last one . . .'

'From your wife?'

'Yes. I didn't get it until very recently, as I was travelling. If I had received it earlier, I would have come sooner.'

They gave him a letter that had been waiting for his arrival. Angel read it rapidly. It was Tess's last letter, short and desperate:

Oh why have you treated me so badly, Angel? I do not deserve it. You are cruel! I intend to forget you. You have been so unfair to me!

T

'It is all quite true!' cried Angel hopelessly, throwing down the letter. 'Perhaps she will never take me back!'

'Angel, don't worry so much about a country girl,' said his mother, anxious about her son's state of mind.

'You know, I've never told you, but she is actually a descendant of one of the oldest, noblest families in England, a d'Urberville in fact. And do you know why I left her? How could I be so narrow-minded! I left her because I discovered she was not the pure country girl I thought. She had been seduced by a so-called gentleman. But it wasn't her fault. And I know now that her whole character is honest and faithful. I must get her back!'

After this outburst Angel went to bed early and thought about the situation. In Brazil it had seemed easy to rush straight back into Tess's loving arms whenever he chose to forgive her. However, now he knew she was angry with him for leaving her for so long. He admitted she was right to be angry. So he decided to give her time to think about their relationship, and wrote to her, at Marlott, instead of going to see her. To his surprise he received in reply a note from her mother.

Dear Sir,
My daughter is not with me at the moment and I don't know when she'll come back. I will let you know when she does. I cannot tell you where she is staying. We don't live in Marlott any more.
                              Yours
                              J. Durbeyfield

At first Clare decided to wait for further information from Tess's mother, but then he re-read the letter sent on to him in Brazil, written from Flintcomb-Ash:

I live only for you. Don't think I shall be bitter because you left me. I am so lonely without you, my darling!
    Haven't you ever felt one little bit of your love for me at the dairy? I am the same woman you fell in love with then, the very same. As soon as I met you, the past was dead for me ...

He was so touched he felt he must go immediately to find her, however angry she and her family might be with him. While he was packing, the letter from Izz and Marian arrived, and made him hurry even more.

His search for Tess took him first to Flintcomb-Ash, where he discovered she had never used her married name. He began to realize, too, what hardship she had suffered rather than ask his family for money. Next he travelled to Marlott, but found the Durbeyfield cottage occupied by others. As he left the village he passed the field where he had first seen Tess at the dance. He could not bear to see it, because Tess was not there. In the churchyard he saw a new headstone, on which was written:

In memory of John Durbeyfield, rightly d'Urberville, of the once powerful family of that name, and direct descendant of Sir Pagan d'Urberville. Died March 10th, 18—

A gravedigger noticed Clare looking at it, and called to him, 'Ah sir, that man didn't want to be buried here, but in his ancestors' tombs at Kingsbere.'

'So why wasn't he buried there?'

'No money. In fact, sir, even this headstone has not been paid for.'

Clare went immediately to pay the bill for the stone, and set out towards Shaston, where he found Mrs Durbeyfield and her children living in a small house. She seemed embarrassed to see him.

'I'm Tess's husband,' he said awkwardly. 'I want to see her at once. You were going to write and tell me where she is. Is she well?'

'I don't know, sir, but *you* ought to.'

'You're right. I ought to know that about my own wife. Where is she?'

Mrs Durbeyfield would not reply.

'Do you think Tess would want me to try and find her?'

'I don't think she would.'

He was turning away, and then he thought of Tess's letter: *If you would come, I could die in your arms! I live only for you . . . I am so lonely without you, my darling!* He turned back.

'I'm sure she would!' he said passionately. 'I know her better than you do!'

'I expect you do, sir, for I have never really known her.'

'Please, Mrs Durbeyfield, please tell me where she is! Please be kind to a miserable lonely man!'

There was a pause after this cry from the heart. Finally Tess's mother replied in a low voice, 'She is at Sandbourne.'

'Thank you,' he said, relieved. 'Do you need anything?'

'No, thank you, sir,' said Joan Durbeyfield. 'We are well provided for.'

Clare took the train to Sandbourne. On his arrival at eleven o'clock in the evening he took a room in a hotel, and walked around the streets, in the hope of meeting Tess. But it was too late to ask anybody.

It seemed a strange place to Clare. It was a bright, fashionable holiday town, with parks, flowerbeds and amusements. This new town, a product of modern civilization, had grown up near the ancient Egdon Woods, where the paths over the hills had not changed for a thousand years.

He walked up and down the wide streets, trying to admire the modern buildings. He felt confused. The sea murmured, and he thought it was the trees. The trees murmured, and he thought it was the sea. He could not understand what had brought Tess here. This was a town for relaxation, for pleasure, not for a working girl like Tess. There were no cows to milk here, and no vegetables to dig. He looked at the lights in the bedroom windows, and wondered which one was hers.

Before going to bed he re-read Tess's passionate letter. He could not sleep that night. At the post office next morning they knew nothing of the names of Clare or Durbeyfield.

'But there is the name of d'Urberville at Mrs Brooks',' said the postman.

'That's it!' cried Clare, pleased to think she had taken her ancestors' name, as he had suggested.

He made his way quickly to Mrs Brooks' house, following the postman's directions. It was a large, impressive house, and he wondered if he should go to the back door, as Tess was probably a servant here. But he rang at the front. Mrs Brooks herself appeared.

'Is Teresa d'Urberville here?' he asked.

'Mrs d'Urberville?'

'Yes.' He felt pleased that she was known there as a married woman. 'Please tell her that a relation wants to see her. Say it's Angel.'

'Mr Angel?'

'No, just Angel. She'll know.'

Angel waited in the sitting room, his heart beating painfully. 'Whatever will she think of me?' he thought. 'I look so different, so much older!' He was still weak after his illness. He could hardly stand, and held on to the back of a chair, as she entered the room.

He was not prepared for what he saw. Tess was wearing fashionable clothes, and looked even more beautiful than he remembered. He had held out his arms, but they fell to his side, because she stood still in the doorway. He thought she could not bear his changed appearance.

'Tess!' he whispered. His voice was low and breaking with emotion. 'Can you forgive me for going away? Can't you . . . come to me? Why are you . . . so beautiful?'

'It is too late,' she said, her voice hard and her eyes shining unnaturally.

'I didn't see you as you really were! Please forgive me, Tessy!' he begged.

'Too late, too late!' she said, waving her hand impatiently. 'Don't come close, Angel! Keep away!'

'But is it that you don't love me, my dear wife, because I've been ill? I've come to find you. My parents will welcome you! I've told them everything!'

'Yes, yes! But it is too late.' Every moment seemed like an hour to her. She felt as if she was in a dream, trying to escape, but unable to. 'Don't you know what has happened? I waited and waited for you. But you didn't come! And I wrote to you, and you didn't come! *He* kept on saying you would never come back again, and he was very kind to my family after father's death. He . . .'

'I don't understand.'

'He has won me back to him.'

Clare stared at her. He saw her fashionable clothes. He saw her relaxed, well-fed body. He saw her white, delicate hands. At last he understood, and fell into a chair, as if hit on the head.

She continued, 'He is upstairs. I hate him now, because he told me a lie, that you would never return, and you *have* returned! Will you go away now, Angel, please, and never come back?'

They looked at each other without joy and without hope, desperately wanting to be sheltered from reality.

'It's my fault!' said Clare. But talking did not help. The Tess he had first loved had separated her body from her soul. Her soul remained and would remain faithful to him for ever. But what happened to her body no longer interested her after he had rejected it.

After a few moments of confused reflection, he realized Tess had left the room. His mind was in a fog. He felt very cold and very ill. Somehow he found himself in the street, walking, although he did not know where.

Mrs Brooks was not usually curious about her guests. She was too interested in the money they paid her, to ask many questions. However, Angel Clare's visit to her wealthy guests, Mr and Mrs d'Urberville, as she knew them, was unusual enough to interest her. She could hear parts of the conversation between the two lost souls, and when Tess went back upstairs, Mrs Brooks crept quietly up to listen outside the bedroom door.

She heard Tess sobbing, and through the keyhole could see her half lying over the breakfast table.

'And then my dear husband came home to me . . . And it's too late! Because you persuaded me, you with your fine words! As you did when you seduced me! You told me he would never come back! But he did! And you helped my family – that's how you persuaded me so cleverly. But when I believed you and came to live with you, he came back! And now I've lost him a second time, and this time for ever! He will hate me now!' She turned her tear-stained face and Mrs Brooks could see how she was suffering. 'And he's dying, he looks as if he's dying! It will be my fault if he dies! You have destroyed my life and his! I can't bear it, I can't!' The man spoke sharply, and after that there was silence.

Mrs Brooks went back downstairs to wait until she was called to take their breakfast away. She could hear Tess moving about, and then saw Tess leave the house, fully dressed in her fashionable clothes. Perhaps Mr d'Urberville was still asleep, as he did not like getting up early. Mrs Brooks wondered who this morning's visitor was, and where Mrs d'Urberville had gone so early.

Just then she noticed a mark on the ceiling. It seemed to be spreading. It was red, and when she stood on the table and touched it, it looked like blood. She ran up to listen at the bedroom door again. The dead silence was broken only by a regular drip, drip, drip. She ran wildly out into the street and begged a man she knew to come back with her. Together they hurried upstairs and pushed open the bedroom door. The breakfast lay untouched on the table, but the large knife was missing. They found it in Alec d'Urberville's heart. He lay on the bed, pale, fixed, dead, still bleeding. Soon the news spread all over Sandbourne that Mrs Brooks' guest had been killed by his young wife.

20

Meanwhile Angel Clare returned to his hotel, and sat for a while over breakfast, staring into space. A note arrived from his mother, saying that his brother Cuthbert was going to marry Mercy Chant. Clare threw away the paper. At last he got up, paid the bill and went to the railway station. But he could not sit patiently and wait for the next train, in an hour's time. He had nothing to wish for in life, and nobody to love. He was in no hurry, but just wanted to get out of that town as soon as possible.

So he started walking along the road out of town. The road was open, and dropped down to cross a valley. When he was climbing the far side of the valley, he stopped for breath, and something made him turn round. There was a small black figure in the distance – a human figure, running. Clare waited. It looked like a woman, but he never imagined that it could be his wife until she came close and he saw it was Tess.

'I saw you – turn on to the road – from the station – and I've been following you all this way!' She was pale, breathless and trembling. He did not question her but took her arm and helped her along. They took a footpath under some trees, to avoid being seen.

'Angel,' she said, 'do you know why I've been running after you? To tell you that I've killed him!' There was a pitiful smile on her white face as she spoke.

'What!' he cried, thinking her mind was disturbed.

'I don't know how I did it,' she said. 'I *had* to do it, for you and me, Angel. I was afraid long ago, when I hit him in the mouth with that heavy glove, that I might kill him one day. He has come between us and ruined our lives. I never loved him at all, Angel. You believe me, don't you? Oh, why did you go away, when I loved you so much? But I don't blame you, Angel. Only, will you forgive me now? I could not bear losing you any longer, I had to kill him. Say you love me now, say you do!'

'Oh, I do love you, Tess, I do. It has all come back!' he said, holding her tightly in his arms. 'But what do you mean, you've killed him?'

'He is dead. He heard me crying about you, and he called you rude names. I couldn't bear it. So I killed him.'

Eventually Angel came to believe that she probably had killed d'Urberville. He was amazed at the strength of her feeling, and this, it seemed, had made her forget the difference between right and wrong. She did not seem to realize what she had done, and laid her head on his shoulder, crying with happiness. He wondered if the bad blood of the d'Urbervilles was to blame for this moment of madness.

However, he knew he could not leave her now. She expected him to protect her. And at last, Clare felt nothing but love for this passionate, loving wife of his. He kissed her again and again, and held her hand.

'I won't leave you! I'll protect you as well as I can, my dearest love, whatever you may or may not have done!'

They walked on, Tess turning her head occasionally to look at him. For her he was still perfection, despite his thinness and pale face. He was the one man who had loved her purely, and who believed in her as pure. Their arms around each other's waists, they walked through the woods on lonely footpaths, taking care not to meet anybody. They did not talk much, being content to be together at last.

'Where shall we go?' asked Tess.

'I don't know. Perhaps we could find a cottage to stay in tonight. Can you walk a long way, Tessy?'

'Oh yes! I could walk for ever with your arm around me!'

At midday Angel went to a public house and brought food and wine back to where Tess was waiting in the woods for him. Her clothes were so fashionable that the country people would have noticed her.

'I think we should keep walking inland, away from the coasts,' said Clare, as they finished eating. 'We can hide there for a while. Later on, when they stop looking for us, we can go to a port and get right out of the country.'

But their plans were vague. They were like two children, who think only of the moment. The weather was warm and they enjoyed walking together. However, in the afternoon they did not find any suitable cottages to stay in, and it was too cold to sleep outside. They had walked about fifteen miles, when they passed a large empty house in the middle of the woods.

'All those rooms empty!' said Tess, 'and we have no shelter!'

'We can stay the night there,' said Clare. 'Look, there's a window open. The caretaker probably airs the rooms in the daytime. We can climb in. Nobody will know.'

And so they did. They chose a bedroom with heavy old-fashioned furniture and a huge old bed. They kept quiet while the caretaker came to shut the windows in the evening. Then the house was theirs. They ate some of the food they had brought, and went to bed in total darkness.

During the night she told him about his sleepwalking just after their wedding.

'You should have told me at the time!'

'Don't think of the past! Think of the present. Tomorrow may mean the end of our happiness.'

But when tomorrow came it was wet and foggy. It seemed that the caretaker only came on fine days, so they were alone in the house. They had enough food and wine, and stayed there

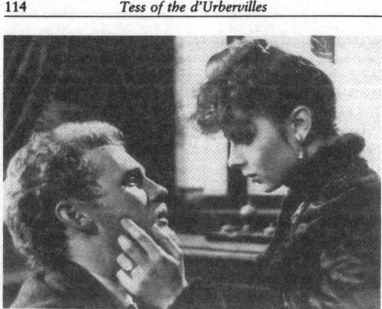

*Inside the house was forgiveness and love: outside was
eventual punishment.*

for the next five days. It was the honeymoon they had never had.
They had no contact with people, and only noticed changes in
the weather. Neither mentioned the depressing period from their
wedding-day to the present. They lived for the moment, and
were completely happy. When Angel suggested leaving their
shelter and travelling to a port like Southampton or London,
Tess was unwilling.

'Why put an end to sweetness and happiness? Outside,
everything is confused and sad. Here, we are quite content.'

Angel agreed. Inside was forgiveness and love: outside was
eventual punishment.

'And . . .' she said, putting her cheek against his, 'I want you
to go on loving me. I'm afraid you might reject me one day for

what I've done. Then I would rather be dead. I must have been mad to kill him! But I don't want to be alive when you reject me for it.'

They stayed for one more day, but the caretaker came early that fine sunny morning. She wanted to open the windows in the bedrooms, which she did not usually do, and opened their bedroom door. She saw the young couple lying in the big bed, fast asleep, and hurried away to tell her neighbours.

Tess and Angel woke soon after, and decided to leave immediately. They dared not stay any longer. When they were in the woods Tess turned to look at the house.

'So much happiness in that house!' she whispered. 'My life can only be a question of a few weeks. Why couldn't we have stayed there?'

'Don't say that, Tess! We'll go northwards and get to a port. They won't find us.'

They kept going all day and most of the night, passing the cathedral city of Melchester and reaching open land. It was a windy, cloudy night. They walked on grass, so as not to make any noise on the road. They were alone and in darkness.

Suddenly, Clare almost bumped into a great stone rising up in front of him. Moving forwards carefully, they found other stones, standing tall and black against the night sky.

'What on earth is this place?' Clare asked.

'Listen!' cried Tess.

The wind, playing on the huge stones, produced a strange tune, like the notes of a great harp. The couple walked slowly into the middle of the great circle of stones.

'It's Stonehenge!' cried Clare.

'The pagan temple?'

'Yes. Older than the centuries; older than the d'Urbervilles!'

'Let's stay here tonight, Angel,' said Tess, lying down on a flat stone which was still warm from the day's sunshine.

'We'd better not. This place can be seen for miles in day-light.'

'I feel at home here,' murmured Tess. 'You used to say at Talbothays that I was a pagan, do you remember?'

He bent over her and kissed her.

'Sleepy, are you, dearest?'

'I love it here,' she said. 'I have been so happy with you. And here I have only the sky above my face. There is nobody in the world except us two.'

Clare thought she could rest a while here. He put his coat over her, and lay down beside her.

'Angel,' she asked presently, as they listened to the wind among the stones, 'if anything happens to me, will you take care of Liza-Lu?'

'I will.'

'She is so good and pure. Oh Angel, I wish you would marry her if you lose me, as you will do soon.'

'If I lose you, I lose everything.'

'She has all the best of me without my bad side, and if she were yours, it would almost seem as if we were not separated by death. Well, I won't mention it again.'

There was silence for a while. Angel could see the first light in the east. They had not much time.

'Did they sacrifice to God here?' she asked.

'No, to the sun.'

'That reminds me, dear. Tell me, do you think we shall meet again after we are dead? I want to know.'

He kissed her to avoid replying.

'Oh Angel, that means no!' she almost sobbed. 'And I so wanted to see you again – so much, so much! Not even you and I, Angel, who love each other so much?'

'This happiness could not have lasted.'

He could not answer. Soon she fell asleep on the stone of sacrifice. The night wind died away, and the stones looked black in the half-light. Something seemed to move in the distance. It was a figure approaching Stonehenge. Clare wished they had gone on, but it was too late. He turned, and saw another, and another. They were uniformed men, closing in on Tess with slow purposeful steps. Clare jumped up wildly, looking round for a way to escape.

'It's no use, sir,' said the nearest policeman. 'We've surrounded the place.'

'Let her finish her sleep!' he begged in a whisper, as the men gathered round the stone. He held her hand. She was breathing more like a trapped animal than a woman. All waited in the growing light, their faces and hands silver, the stones grey. When the light was strong, she awoke.

'What is it, Angel?' she said, sitting up. 'Have they come for me?'

'Yes, dearest, they have.'

'That is right. I am almost glad. This happiness could not have lasted!'

She stood up and went towards the waiting men. 'I am ready,' she said quietly.

One July morning the sun shone on two figures climbing the hill leading out of the fine city of Wintoncester. They were young but they walked bent in sorrow. One was Angel Clare, the other Tess's younger sister, Liza-Lu. Hand in hand, with pale, tear-stained faces, they walked in silence.

When they reached the top of the hill, they heard the town clocks strike eight. They turned quickly and looked back at the city. They could see the cathedral, the college and the prison very clearly. A tall post was fixed to the prison tower. A few minutes after eight, as they watched, a black flag moved slowly up the post.

The gods had finished playing with Tess. Society had seen 'justice' done. Her d'Urberville ancestors slept on in their tombs, uncaring. The two silent watchers dropped to the ground and stayed there without moving for a long time. The flag waved in the wind. As soon as they had strength, they stood up, joined hands again, and continued slowly on their way.

GLOSSARY

affection fondness; gentle, lasting love (as of a parent for a child)

ancestors members of a family who lived a long time ago

ashes what is left of a fire which is no longer burning

baptize to perform the ceremony of receiving someone (often a baby) into the Christian Church

bear *(v)* to suffer pain or unhappiness

beehive a home for bees (insects which produce honey)

blush *(v)* to become red in the face, especially when embarrassed

bull a male cow; a large, often dangerous animal

caretaker someone who is paid to look after an empty house

cathedral a large, important church

cheek the side of the face below the eye

churn *(n)* a container in which milk is stirred to make butter

cock a male chicken, with brightly coloured feathers, and a loud call which is usually heard very early in the morning

corn various grassy plants grown in fields and used to make flour

county one of the regions that a country is divided into

crow *(n)* to make a noise like a cock (some country people believe that if a new husband hears a cock crow, it means his wife is not pure, not a virgin)

dairy a place where milk is kept and butter and cream are made

descendant a person with an old, well-known family as ancestors

desire *(n)* a strong wish

destined intended or planned in advance (by God or fate)

drunk *(n)* a person who has drunk too much and cannot control his actions

faithful loyal to somebody for a long time; keeping promises to stay with your wife/husband

flour-mill a building with machinery to make flour from corn

garlic a plant (wild or from gardens) with a strong taste and smell

give way to allow oneself to be overcome or beaten by something

gentleman (in this story) a man of good family, usually wealthy

grasshopper an insect that jumps and makes a sharp sound by rubbing its back legs together (often heard in the countryside in summer)

greenhouse a glass building used for growing delicate plants

harp a large musical stringed instrument, in the shape of a triangle

hedge a line of small trees planted close together

holy of God; religious

honeymoon a short holiday for a newly-married couple

honour *(n)* good, respected personal character and behaviour

instinct a natural reaction; a force in people which makes them behave in a certain way

justice the quality or ideal of being right and fair

logic a way of reasoning or thinking systematically

maiden an old-fashioned word for a girl who is a virgin (with no experience of sex with a man)

mistletoe an evergreen plant, often hung in a house at Christmas (there is an old custom of kissing under the mistletoe)

noble *(adj)* of a good, often ancient family with a high social position

pagan *(adj)* of a person who is not a believer in any of the world's main religions

parson a priest in charge of a small area

passion strong feeling or emotion, especially of love, hate or anger

philosophy the study of beliefs and ideas

preacher a religious person (not always a priest) who gives talks about religion, good behaviour, etc.

public house a place where alcoholic drinks are bought and drunk

reap *(v)* to cut the corn when it is ready

reject *(v)* to refuse to accept

ribbon a small thin piece of coloured material worn in the hair

ruin *(v)* to destroy or spoil; *(n)* a building which has fallen down or been destroyed

seal *(n)* a stamp or ring with the family name or sign

seduce to persuade someone (usually young and inexperienced) against their wishes to have sex

shed *(n)* a building for farm animals

shilling a British coin no longer in use

skim *(v)* to remove the cream (the richer milk) from the milk

sob *(v)* to cry loudly and very unhappily

stool a small seat without a back

strawberry a small, red, juicy, soft fruit

suicide a person who kills him/herself

symbol a thing that represents or suggests something

temple a building used for religious purpose

threshing-machine a machine for beating or rubbing corn to separate the best part from the outer covering

title a word for people of noble family (e.g. Lord, Prince)

tomb a box-like container made of stone, for dead bodies in a church or churchyard

tragic very, very sad and unfortunate

vague uncertain; unclear

waggon an open cart or carriage pulled by a horse

Tess of the d'Urbervilles

ACTIVITIES

ACTIVITIES

Before Reading

1 Read the story introduction on the first page of the book, and the back cover. Which of these sentences are true?

   1 Tess comes from a poor family.
   2 She has had a good education.
   3 A rich young man falls in love with her.
   4 People say she is to blame for what happens.
   5 She has a very happy life.

2 What was life like for poor country girls a hundred years ago? Discuss your answers to these questions.

   1 What kind of work was available for uneducated women?

farm work	paid housework
factory work	teaching
looking after children	office work
nursing	working for the government

   2 Which was more important for most women in those days, finding a job or finding a husband?

3 What do you think will happen in the story? Circle Y (yes) or N (no) for each sentence.

   1 Tess will marry the wrong man. Y/N
   2 Tess will die for love. Y/N
   3 Tess will lose her beauty, and become old and ugly. Y/N
   4 Men will fight over her, and die for her. Y/N
   5 Her death will change people's lives. Y/N

ACTIVITIES

While Reading

Read Chapters 1 to 5, and then answer these questions.

1 What had Parson Tringham discovered about the Durbeyfields?
2 What was the countryside round Marlott like?
3 Why was Tess sad at the May-Day dance?
4 What illness was John Durbeyfield suffering from?
5 Why were the Durbeyfield family so poor?
6 Why did Tess have to take the beehives to market?
7 How did the accident happen to Prince and the waggon?
8 Why did Joan Durbeyfield want Tess to visit old Mrs
   d'Urberville at Trantridge?
9 What made Tess agree to go there?
10 How much was John Durbeyfield prepared to sell his title for?
11 Why was Tess alone with Alec in the woods at night?

**Read Chapters 6 and 7. Choose the best question-word for these
questions, and then answer the questions.**

What / Why / How

1 . . . did Alec d'Urberville mean by 'I am ready to pay for it'?
2 . . . did Tess feel about Alec?
3 . . . did Joan Durbeyfield react when she heard Tess's story?
4 . . . was Tess's attitude to her child, according to the village
   women?
5 . . . couldn't Tess have her baby baptized by the parson?
6 . . . did Tess do, to save her baby from hell?
7 . . . did Tess decide to leave Marlott?

Read Chapters 8 to 11. Are these sentences true (T) or false (F)? Rewrite the false sentences with the correct information.

1 Tess was delighted to leave home for the second time.
2 She felt little respect for her noble ancestors.
3 Like her father, she wanted to work hard and be independent.
4 Tess and Angel recognized each other at once, from the May-Day dance a few years before.
5 Angel's parents did not send him to university, because he was not clever enough.
6 Tess's occasional sadness made her more attractive to Angel.
7 She gladly accepted Angel's offer to help her study.
8 She was unable to forget about her past experience.
9 She could not bear the idea of Angel falling in love with any of the other dairymaids.
10 Common sense overcame passion, when Angel first spoke of love to Tess.

Read Chapters 12 and 13. Look at these questions asked, or considered, by Angel and Tess. Answer them in your own words and with your own ideas.

ANGEL
1 Ought he to marry Tess?
2 What would his mother and brothers say, if he married her?
3 What would he himself say two years after the wedding?
4 What sort of wife does a farmer need?
5 What is the advantage of marrying a 'lady', a girl of good family?
6 Should his wife be educated, like Mercy Chant, or should he choose 'a wife from nature, not from civilization'?

TESS

1 Ought she to marry Angel?

2 How would his parents react?

3 Could she make him happy?

4 Would anyone tell him about her past?

5 Should she tell him the truth, and if so, should she tell him before or after the wedding?

6 If she told him everything, would he forgive her?

Before you read Chapters 14 to 16, can you guess how the story will develop? Choose one of these possibilities.

1 Angel will forgive Tess, as she has forgiven him.

2 Angel will be angry, and will divorce Tess or send her away.

3 Tess will leave Angel, because she thinks she really belongs to Alec d'Urberville.

4 Angel will search for Alec d'Urberville, and be killed by him.

5 Tess will feel so guilty about her past that she will kill herself.

Read Chapters 14 to 20. Who said or wrote this to whom? What, or who, were they talking about?

1 'You are so childish! You don't understand the law.'

2 'She would have laid down her life for you.'

3 'I'm afraid of your power over me.'

4 'Why am I on the wrong side of this stone?'

5 'A woman's strength cannot last for ever.'

6 'Oh, it's not the Angel who went away!'

7 'I didn't see you as you really were!'

8 'Let her finish her sleep!'

9 'This happiness could not have lasted.'

ACTIVITIES

After Reading

1 Tess wrote to her mother, asking for advice about whether to tell Angel the truth about her past (see her mother's reply on page 61). Write Tess's letter, using these prompts to help you.

Dear Mother,
- hope all well at home / children
- exciting news / getting married / future husband / gentleman
- urgent question to ask you / reply quickly
- tell him about my past? / want to be honest / start married life
- love him very much / lose him?
- not sure what to do / very worried / please help!

Your loving daughter, Tess

Would *you* have given Tess the advice her mother gave her? Why, or why not?

2 This is a story of mistakes that were made and opportunities that were missed. What might have happened if . . .? Complete these sentences in your own words.

1 If Angel had danced with Tess in the May-Day dance, . . .
2 If Alec d'Urberville hadn't seduced Tess, . . .
3 If Tess's baby had lived, . . .
4 If Tess hadn't told Angel about her past, . . .
5 If Tess had met Angel's parents, instead of his brothers, . . .
6 If Angel had come back from Brazil sooner, . . .
7 If Tess hadn't killed Alec d'Urberville, . . .

3 Angel Clare discussed his problems with a man he met in Brazil (see pages 97/98). Complete Angel's part of the conversation.

STRANGER: So, tell me, why are you separated from your wife?
ANGEL: _____
STRANGER: Travelling's dangerous for *anyone* in this country! That's not the real reason, is it?
ANGEL: _____
STRANGER: What kind of mistake? You mean you married the wrong girl?
ANGEL: _____
STRANGER: But if she's so beautiful, why aren't you with her now?
ANGEL: _____
STRANGER: Poor girl! That wasn't her fault though, was it?
ANGEL: _____
STRANGER: Purity and innocence! You expected too much, my friend. So what did you do when you discovered she had a past?
ANGEL: _____
STRANGER: What? You left your wife just because of something that happened years ago, which she couldn't even prevent!
ANGEL: _____
STRANGER: Well, if I were you, I'd go straight home. Ask her to forgive you – you still have a chance of happiness together.
ANGEL: _____
STRANGER: She might. She sounds as if she has a loving nature. But you've behaved very badly to her, you realize that!
ANGEL: _____
STRANGER: Say that to her, just as you've said it to me. And if she runs into your arms, you'll be a luckier man than you deserve to be!

4 After Tess's arrest, she was sent for trial at Wintoncester. Complete
   the speech for the prosecution with the words below.

   decides, demand, dies, face, fortunately, heart, hides, husband,
   innocent, law, lover, married, murder, must, punishment, simple,
   stabs, stolen, tired, wealthy

   'My lord, this is a _____ matter of _____. A young woman, who is
   living with a _____ gentleman, although she is not _____ to him,
   _____ to put an end to the relationship. We do not know why –
   perhaps she has _____ of him and found a new _____, or perhaps
   she has _____ money from him. She takes a sharp knife and _____
   it deep into his _____. The gentleman _____ instantly, and the
   woman realizes she _____ run away, to escape _____. So she
   _____ in the countryside, with the help of her _____, who has
   recently returned from Brazil. But _____, the forces of _____ and
   order find her in the end, and bring her back to _____ trial. I _____
   justice for the death of an _____ man! Tess Durbeyfield must die!'

5 Now complete the speech for the defence. Put the phrases or
   sentences in the right order. Then, using these linking words, join
   the sentences together to make a paragraph of five sentences.

   therefore / and / because / and when / as soon as / later / who /
   however

   1 At the age of sixteen, she met the wealthy Mr d'Urberville,
   2 she picked up a knife and stabbed her lover through the heart.
   3 . . . , she fell in love with and married this gentleman, Angel
      Clare,
   4 . . . she has already suffered enough!

5 . . . he found out about her past.

6 My lord, let me remind you of this poor girl's history.

7 . . . was seduced by him.

8 . . . Tess realized that d'Urberville was spoiling her chance of happiness with her much-loved husband,

9 . . . , my lord, I say she does not deserve to die for a moment of madness,

10 . . . chose to live apart from her

11 He returned, . . . , after some years abroad, only to find her living with d'Urberville,

6 **Do you agree (A) or disagree (D) with these statements? Explain why.**

1 The parson was right to tell John Durbeyfield about his connection with the d'Urbervilles.

2 Tess could have prevented Alec from seducing her.

3 Angel's and Tess's guilty secrets were the same.

4 Tess was as pure at the end of the story as at the beginning.

5 Angel Clare did more to destroy Tess than Alec did.

6 The whole tragedy was no one's fault.

7 **Now discuss these more general statements, with reference to the story.**

1 A mother always knows best.

2 Honesty is the best policy.

3 Love is blind.

4 We are masters of our own destinies.

5 Where there's life, there's hope.

ABOUT THE AUTHOR

Thomas Hardy (1840–1928) was born in the village of Higher Bockhampton in Dorset, in the south of England. He loved the old ways and traditions of country life, which had been such an important part of his childhood and family background. His father, a stonemason, led the singing in the church choir, and gave his son both an interest in church architecture and a feeling for music. After attending local schools until he was sixteen, Hardy became the pupil of a Dorchester church architect. His mother encouraged him to continue his wider studies, so he went on reading Latin and Greek in the evenings.

At twenty-two, he went to London to work as an architect, and it was here that he started writing. When he found that publishers did not want his poetry, he turned to novels, and wrote one a year from 1871 to 1875. The most popular of these was *Far from the Madding Crowd*, which came out in 1874, and its success meant that he could not only give up architecture and concentrate on writing, but also afford to get married. He continued to produce short stories and novels, including *The Trumpet Major*, *The Mayor of Casterbridge* and *The Woodlanders*, which were received with great enthusiasm by the public. However, when *Tess of the d'Urbervilles* was published in 1891, it was criticized for its tragic ending and its description of the harsh realities of life for poor country people. And when *Jude the Obscure* came out in 1896, both critics and the general public protested strongly at the despair and hopelessness surrounding the horrifying, though believable, events in the story. After this attack on his work, Hardy gave up writing novels completely; he returned to his first love, poetry, and during the last thirty years of his life published eight volumes of verse.

Many people admire Hardy for his novels, which describe the countryside and its people so well. Most of the stories are set in Dorset, where he was born, and describe farming techniques and country customs in careful, loving detail. Other readers prefer his poems, which range over life and death, love and loss, age and youth, peace and war. A number of his poems written after 1914 reflect his feelings of sadness and guilt at the death of his first wife, although by this time he had married again.

It was Hardy's experience of country life that supplied most of the material for his writing, and he continued to draw on childhood memories throughout his long writing life. Like many country people, he was a fatalist, and believed that whatever happens in life must simply be accepted. But, as we can see in *Tess of the d'Urbervilles*, he did not approve of the strict code of moral behaviour which society demanded in his time, because he thought it did not allow for natural feelings or mistakes. He was a realist, and wanted to describe people, situations, and problems as they really existed, right up to their tragic end, as in *Jude the Obscure*. But today, most people read Hardy's novels for their great themes of love and tragedy, their moving language, and their beautiful descriptions of the English countryside as it used to be.

Hardy's stories, with their clear storyline, varied characters, rich language and identifiable background, have always attracted film-makers. The photographs in this book are from a film of *Tess of the d'Urbervilles*, and there have been recent films of *Jude the Obscure* and *The Woodlanders*.

OXFORD BOOKWORMS LIBRARY

Classics • Crime & Mystery • Factfiles • Fantasy & Horror
Human Interest • Playscripts • Thriller & Adventure
True Stories • World Stories

The OXFORD BOOKWORMS LIBRARY provides enjoyable reading in English, with a wide range of classic and modern fiction, non-fiction, and plays. It includes original and adapted texts in seven carefully graded language stages, which take learners from beginner to advanced level. An overview is given on the next pages.

All Stage 1 titles are available as audio recordings, as well as over eighty other titles from Starter to Stage 6. All Starters and many titles at Stages 1 to 4 are specially recommended for younger learners. Every Bookworm is illustrated, and Starters and Factfiles have full-colour illustrations.

The OXFORD BOOKWORMS LIBRARY also offers extensive support. Each book contains an introduction to the story, notes about the author, a glossary, and activities. Additional resources include tests and worksheets, and answers for these and for the activities in the books. There is advice on running a class library, using audio recordings, and the many ways of using Oxford Bookworms in reading programmes. Resource materials are available on the website <www.oup.com/bookworms>.

The *Oxford Bookworms Collection* is a series for advanced learners. It consists of volumes of short stories by well-known authors, both classic and modern. Texts are not abridged or adapted in any way, but carefully selected to be accessible to the advanced student.

You can find details and a full list of titles in the *Oxford Bookworms Library Catalogue* and *Oxford English Language Teaching Catalogues*, and on the website <www.oup.com/bookworms>.

THE OXFORD BOOKWORMS LIBRARY
GRADING AND SAMPLE EXTRACTS

STARTER • 250 HEADWORDS

present simple – present continuous – imperative –
can/cannot, must – *going to* (future) – simple gerunds ...

Her phone is ringing – but where is it?

Sally gets out of bed and looks in her bag. No phone. She looks under the bed. No phone. Then she looks behind the door. There is her phone. Sally picks up her phone and answers it. *Sally's Phone*

STAGE 1 • 400 HEADWORDS

... past simple – coordination with *and, but, or* –
subordination with *before, after, when, because, so* ...

I knew him in Persia. He was a famous builder and I worked with him there. For a time I was his friend, but not for long. When he came to Paris, I came after him – I wanted to watch him. He was a very clever, very dangerous man. *The Phantom of the Opera*

STAGE 2 • 700 HEADWORDS

... present perfect – *will* (future) – *(don't) have to, must not, could* –
comparison of adjectives – simple *if* clauses – past continuous –
tag questions – *ask/tell* + infinitive ...

While I was writing these words in my diary, I decided what to do. I must try to escape. I shall try to get down the wall outside. The window is high above the ground, but I have to try. I shall take some of the gold with me – if I escape, perhaps it will be helpful later. *Dracula*

STAGE 3 • 1000 HEADWORDS
... should, may – present perfect continuous – *used to* – past perfect –
causative – relative clauses – indirect statements ...

Of course, it was most important that no one should see
Colin, Mary, or Dickon entering the secret garden. So Colin
gave orders to the gardeners that they must all keep away
from that part of the garden in future. *The Secret Garden*

STAGE 4 • 1400 HEADWORDS
*... past perfect continuous – passive (simple forms) –
would* conditional clauses – indirect questions –
relatives with *where/when* – gerunds after prepositions/phrases ...

I was glad. Now Hyde could not show his face to the world
again. If he did, every honest man in London would be proud
to report him to the police. *Dr Jekyll and Mr Hyde*

STAGE 5 • 1800 HEADWORDS
... future continuous – future perfect –
passive (modals, continuous forms) –
would have conditional clauses – modals + perfect infinitive ...

If he had spoken Estella's name, I would have hit him. I was so
angry with him, and so depressed about my future, that I could
not eat the breakfast. Instead I went straight to the old house.
Great Expectations

STAGE 6 • 2500 HEADWORDS
... passive (infinitives, gerunds) – advanced modal meanings –
clauses of concession, condition

When I stepped up to the piano, I was confident. It was as if I
knew that the prodigy side of me really did exist. And when I
started to play, I was so caught up in how lovely I looked that
I didn't worry how I would sound. *The Joy Luck Club*